The Mexican American Community College Experience

The Mexican American Community College Experience

Fostering Resilience, Achieving Success

Blanca Campa

AMERICAN
ASSOCIATION OF
COMMUNITY
COLLEGES

ROWMAN & LITTLEFIELD
Lanham • Boulder • New York • London

A grateful acknowledgment is made to the following for permission to use material:

Routledge Taylor and Francis Group: Excerpts from "Pedagogies of Survival: Cultural Resources to Foster Resilience Among Mexican-American Community College Students" in *Community College Journal of Research and Practice*, copyright © Taylor and Francis Group by Blanca Campa.

Sage Publications: Excerpts from "Critical Resilience, Schooling Processes and the Academic Success of Mexican Americans in a Community College" in *Hispanic Journal of Behavioral Sciences*, copyright © Blanca Campa.

Published by Rowman & Littlefield
A wholly owned subsidary of The Rowman & Littlefield Publishing Group, Inc.
4501 Forbes Boulevard, Suite 200, Lanham, Maryland 20706
www.rowman.com

Unit A, Whitacre Mews, 26-34 Stannary Street, London SE11 4AB

British Library Cataloguing in Publication Information Available

Library of Congress Cataloging-in-Publication Data is Available

ISBN 978-1-4758-3406-2 (cloth: alk. paper)
ISBN 978-1-4758-3407-9 (pbk: alk. paper)
ISBN 978-1-4758-3408-6 (electronic)

∞ ™ The paper used in this publication meets the minimum requirements of American National Standard for Information Sciences Permanence of Paper for Printed Library Materials, ANSI/NISO Z39.48-1992.

Printed in the United States of America

Contents

Foreword

It is my pleasure to introduce Dr. Blanca Campa's inspirational work, *The Mexican American Community College Experience: Fostering Resilience, Achieving Success*, published by Rowman & Littlefield and the American Association of Community Colleges (AACC). The experiences described in the book highlight and exemplify El Paso Community College's (EPCC's) teaching, learning, and student success initiatives and demonstrate the importance of community colleges serving diverse students across America.

EPCC fills a vital role as a progressive educational leader offering access to both high-quality and affordable academic opportunities that contributes to the border community. With an unwavering focus on success for all students, EPCC prepares individuals to achieve their current academic goals, meet tomorrow's challenges, and be competitive in local and global job markets. This book celebrates resilience, achievement, and innovation and is testament to the college's commitment to students and the borderland community.

In this book, Campa, who initially joined EPCC as a counselor and later became a professor in Educational Psychology, describes the rapid growth of the Hispanic population in the United States in recent decades and explains how community colleges have become an integral part of their pursuit of the American Dream. With her eclectic background in education, counseling, and psychology combined with her doctorate in Curriculum and Instruction, she brings important research, observations, and perspectives to the field. She presents an interesting overview of community colleges and their history, evolution, and development.

The first chapter describes the challenges faced by these institutions and how so much of our work is "hidden," understudied, unknown, and unappreciated. Campa points out that when community colleges are examined, they are often studied by outsiders (university professors, researchers, or graduate students), thus realizing the importance of exploring community colleges from the inside.

As a result, she began to conduct her own studies by working with students in Education 1300, the college's freshman experience course. She found the course to be an essential component of the college's curriculum, a gateway course that prepares students for college studies, refreshes basic skills, and places emphasis on career planning. In the process, she discovered that through this important course, our students often learn much about themselves, develop goals and strategies, and begin to see their larger purpose in the world.

The Mexican American Community College Experience looks far beyond the freshman experience and explores the "unknown" world of the community college classroom. We meet resilient teachers who have often faced barriers and obstacles in their own lives and now help our students pursue their goals and dreams. Unique classroom and community experiences guided by energetic, committed faculty help them develop skills, explore new interests, and accumulate the social and cultural capital needed to achieve success in college and in their lives. By building resilience, EPCC helps students improve their personal quality of life and eventually contribute to their economically and culturally diverse community, the primary missions of the college.

By her descriptive analysis of methods of classroom pedagogy and engagement, we see students learning about their neighborhoods, connecting or reconnecting to their families, and finding a greater world off campus where they hope to make contributions. The classrooms she describes are comfortable, nurturing environments in which standards are high and students are expected to perform.

The Mexican American Community College Experience highlights numerous EPCC faculty and programs. It features some of the EPCC's many creative efforts that enhance student resilience, learning, growth, achievement, and success. It describes a variety of experiences in service learning, the Puente Program, learning communities, remedial instruction, and community engagement.

The Mexican American Community College Experience is well grounded in education and psychology theory, showing how resilience can be developed and nurtured. The book features many personal stories that illustrate the challenges, struggles, and successes of EPCC students. It explores culture, community, and family. We learn how committed professors strive for improvement and prepare our EPCC students for success, achievement, and fulfillment.

Campa's *The Mexican American Community College Experience* helps explain much of the success of the El Paso Community College district in recent years.

On average, our committed faculty and staff annually serve more than 35,000 students enrolled in academic, workforce training and continuing education programs at five campuses located throughout El Paso County. The college offers cutting-edge technology, ultramodern training facilities, and numerous innovative learning options. A sixth campus, located at the U.S. Army's Fort Bliss, scheduled to be built in 2020, will be a unique collaboration with the University of Texas at El Paso, New Mexico State University, and others, the first collaboration of its kind at one of the largest military installations in the United States.

EPCC has been ranked by both *Hispanic Outlook Magazine* and *Community College Week* as first among nearly 1,200 community colleges in awarding associate degrees to Hispanic students and sixteenth of all colleges and universities; EPCC was awarded the 2013 Higher Education Excellence in Diversity (HEED) award from *INSIGHT into Diversity* magazine, the oldest and largest diversity-focused publication in higher education. EPCC is consistently named to the coveted Military Friendly Schools list, which recognizes the top colleges, universities, and trade schools in the country that are doing the most to embrace America's military service members, veterans, and spouses as students and ensure their success on campus.

In 2015 the Aspen Institute named EPCC as one of ten nationwide finalists for the Aspen Prize for community college excellence, which recognizes a college's impact on student success. EPCC was selected competitively from community colleges across the nation based on measurable excellence in four areas: learning, degree completion, employment and earnings, and success for minority and low-income students.

EPCC continues to be recognized for its commitment to students and to our community. The college received the AACC Student Success Award of Excellence in 2016 and was awarded a Regional Equity Award by ACCT for promoting diversity and inclusion. EPCC has also been recognized nationally as an Achieving the Dream Leader College, is a previous recipient of the Leah Meyer Austin Institutional Student Success Leadership Award for outstanding institutional achievement, and has been recognized by Excelencia in Education with the "Examples of Excelencia" Award for the Early College High School Program.

In 2015 EPCC was competitively selected as one of only thirty colleges across the nation to participate in the AACC Pathways Project, a national project funded by the Bill and Melinda Gates Foundation that focuses on building capacity for community colleges to design and implement better structured academic and career pathways for all students.

EPCC continues to build community partnerships throughout the region with increased emphasis on early college and dual credit programs for the public school systems in order to provide more educational opportunities to high school students throughout El Paso County. With the commitment and dedication of our faculty, we will continue to build resilience and promote student success and achievement. In the future, EPCC will continue our focus on engaging students, growing community partnerships, and fostering a culture of excellence with measurable success. By creating a college-going culture and innovative student success initiatives, EPCC is opening the pathway to higher education and a better prepared workforce in our region.

—William Serrata, PhD, president, El Paso Community College

Acknowledgments

I am indebted to many people for their help and encouragement throughout this exciting process. They validated my work, gave me a greater sense of purpose, and helped me build my own resilience.

The El Paso Community College professors who participated in the research are a good place to start: Joe Old, Rose Galindo, Dr. Myshie Pagel, Richard Yañez, Lolo Mercado, Lisa McNiel, and many others. I thank them for trusting me with their stories, providing me with their precious time, inspiring me with their amazing abilities to teach *con respeto*, and supporting the interests that I am so passionate about. A special thanks goes to Professor Heather Oesterreich (Dr. O) of New Mexico State University (NMSU), who introduced me to feminist critical theory. My gratitude also goes out to the other members of my dissertation committee, Dr. Kyle Shanton, Dr. Elsa Arroyos-Jurado, and Dr. Kimberly Oliver, for guiding me through the dissertation process that gave birth to the ideas in this book.

I would also like to express my sincere appreciation to Dr. Rudolfo Chávez Chávez and the late Dr. Peggy Glaister Kaczmarek for mentoring me and for introducing me to exciting literature. A special thanks to my NMSU research partners, Kathleen Garcia and Sandra Nakamura, whose love and support I will always cherish.

Even though my academic preparation was an important part of this journey, the teachings of my student participants were the most enlightening part of the process. I have gained a deep profound respect for them and have learned more than I could have ever imagined about resilience. This book is a compilation of original research and a review of literature in various fields related to resilience, community colleges, Mexican Americans, and student achievement. The book is based on direct observations, formal and informal interviews, and a variety of written materials. The views, analysis, and opinions expressed or implied are solely my own, based on and inspired by the remarkable students, faculty, and staff at El Paso Community College.

I owe much to my editor Sarah Jubar at Rowman & Littlefield. Sarah was the first to recognize the value of my ideas and helped to launch them. Her professionalism, support, and excitement made this work a reality.

I would also like to generously thank the American Association of Community Colleges (AACC) for serving as a co-publisher of this book.

I thank Dr. Amado Padilla from Stanford University for believing in my work and helping me publish my first article on resilience. In addition, I also thank my friends and colleagues at El Paso Community College: Keith Pannell, Tony Procell, Jose Baltazar, Deans Jaime Farias, Julie Penley, Vice President of Research and Accountability Saul Candelas, and President William Serrata for supporting my work.

I wish to thank my dear mentor, Joe Old, whose tremendous excitement and support carried me through this process. Joe meticulously read every page of my dissertation and several chapters of this book, offering countless suggestions and revisions. My mothers, Manuela Valdez, Josefa Bermudez, Dorothy Torok, and Andrea Lozano, and my fathers, Miguel Campa, Eduardo Campa, Francisco Campa, Luis Granillo, and George D. Torok Sr., inspire me, and they are the soul of this work. I also thank all the members of my family who I try to lift as I climb. I thank my nephew, Angel Arturo Garcia, who is now one of my many guardian angels.

Finally, I send my love and gratitude to my beautiful son Jorge Campa-Torok, who motivates and inspires me every day, and to my husband, Dr. George D. Torok. They are the heart of this work. George's love, sweat, and inspiration are visible on every page. He has been my constant companion and intellectual cheerleader throughout the last twenty years and will no doubt be so forever.

—Blanca Campa, PhD, El Paso, Texas

Introduction

If there was anyone left in the United States who was still unaware of how dramatically the Latino population has grown in recent decades, the 2016 presidential election has by now enlightened and perhaps even shocked them. Latinos comprise the largest ethnic minority group in the United States, constituting 16 percent of the nation's population, and their rate of growth continues to rise. In some parts of the United States, Latinos will constitute the majority population as well as a majority of the electorate in the coming decades (Ennis, Rio-Vargas, and Albert 2011).

Although they were once a small portion of the general population (less than 2 percent in 1960), Latinos now reside in every state and are represented in almost every community in the country. Once concentrated in the border regions and states such as Texas, California, and Florida, they have now settled in Midwestern farming communities, small cities in the Northeast, and throughout the South. As the diaspora has expanded and numbers have grown, Latinos now occupy distinguished positions in the fields of politics, government, business, finance, and entertainment. They have become doctors, lawyers, school teachers, and successful entrepreneurs. The Latino influence can be clearly seen in our popular culture, cuisine, and politics. In many places, it appears that Latinos have made their way in through the assimilation process and are achieving the American Dream.

But there is another side to this story in which Latinos can fall behind throughout the process and suffer disproportionally from unemployment, limited opportunities, and poverty when compared to the general population. Even though Latinos make up one-fourth of public school students and are making some progress, they continue to lag behind other racial and ethnic groups in terms of educational achievements (Lopez and Fry 2013). They are less likely to complete a bachelor's degree, causing them to be further under-represented in graduate and professional programs (Lopez and Fry 2013).

Much of the growth in the Latino population is quite recent, having taken place within the past fifty years. Most come from a few select places, such as Mexico, Cuba, the Central American nations, and territorial Puerto Rico. Often unskilled and uneducated, Latinos tend to work in low-paying jobs with few opportunities for advancement (Fry 2002; Melguizo 2009).

Traditionally, immigrant populations move up through the new social strata with each generation. But overall, the Latino population often appears stuck, unable to break out of the cycle. This places the burden on the younger generations to succeed and advance, yet the nation's young Latino population—who will comprise a substantial percentage of the workforce by 2025—are plagued by low educational achievement in a world that increasingly requires more skills and knowledge for success (Fry 2002; Melguizo 2009). Limited education, underachievement, underrepresentation, and low incomes in the Latino community have been well documented and remain one of the great challenges of the twenty-first century.

And yet within this context many are able to succeed. Their perseverance and resilience allow them to overcome obstacles and move through the system toward that elusive American Dream. I have been observing and researching this phenomenon for almost fifteen years while teaching a first-year experience, or college freshman course, for students entering El Paso Community College. The course helps prepare them for further college studies and develops various life skills that allow them to move forward, often while facing tremendous obstacles.

My laboratory is the United States–Mexico border, a thriving but often unstable environment plagued by poverty and violence. My students are predominantly Mexican and Mexican American, who now comprise 63 percent of the Latino population. (I use the term *Mexican American* without the hyphen because it is a single and fluid concept.) In my classes, I have met many students who faced adversities but demonstrated high levels of resilience and ultimately achieved extraordinary outcomes.

Latinos often find the transition into higher education an overwhelming experience (Rendón, García, and Person 2004). They have already survived varying forms of poverty, racism, gender discrimination, and marginalization. When coupled with learning English as a Second Language (ESL), the task becomes even more challenging and, in some cases, traumatic. Many of these students have attended public schools with minimal standards, low expectations, and substandard teaching (Melguizo 2009).

In addition, they may come from homes in which going to college conflicts with the established cultural traditions. For many, just the act of attending school is a struggle. They navigate through many barriers, particularly if they are from working-class backgrounds or are the first in their family to attend college. Some scholars argue that as students endure various forms of struggle, they develop important attributes that allow them to move within and between multiple worlds and maneuver around these barriers (Campa 2010; Rendón, García, and Person 2004).

Given that these students have already navigated around many obstacles and have worked their way into community colleges and universities, it is of utmost importance that their college experiences help them achieve their goals and aspirations (Rendón, García, and Person 2004). It is these students and their heroic journeys that have motivated and inspired me over the years.

I have explored their worlds and attempted to understand how they and other Mexican American community college students who experience similar adversities develop and sustain the resilience that helps them achieve their goals. So despite beginning with a somewhat discouraging introduction, this book is not about failure. It is about resilience, the ability to work around obstacles, break through barriers, and ultimately move forward.

A BRIEF OVERVIEW

Community colleges play an increasingly important role in building the resilience of Mexican and Mexican American students whose presence on campuses around the country has added a new dynamic dimension to American higher education. Community colleges attract all types of students but are particularly appealing to Latinos. These students are more likely to enroll in a community college than students from any other racial or ethnic minority group (Krogstad 2015; Martinez and Fernández 2004). More than half of Latinos, and Mexican Americans in particular, enter higher education through a community college (Krogstad 2015; Kurlaender 2006).

In fact, minority students, who only represent 21 percent of all the students in higher education, make up 60 percent of those attending community colleges (Martinez and Fernández 2004). This places community colleges in a unique position to facilitate the success of minority students. These institutions are now an important part of the American educational landscape and play a crucial role in shaping the lives of Mexican Americans who eventually transfer to four-year colleges, graduate with a bachelor's degree, and go beyond. Hence they are certainly worthy of more in-depth study and analysis.

This book describes resilient Mexican American community college students and their supportive, resilient professors. Their stories come from four research case studies that covered a time span of ten years and included approximately fifty participants (see the appendix). This book provides the reader with a description of resilience based on research in psychology and some reconceptualization of this construct from a critical feminist perspective. The diverse experiences of the students and professors are used to describe resilience and how it is developed.

In addition, this book offers the reader principles, perspectives, and methods used by professors to cultivate the resilience of their students. The community college provides the setting, a place where these people come together and, consciously or unconsciously, foster resilience. In many cases, the very professors who are building student resilience are not even aware of the contributions they are making.

This book is a combination of research and narrative or "qualitative research and lived reality" (Ladson-Billings 1994, x). It integrates description, reflection, and scholarship. The four following voices are present in my work: that of a Mexican American researcher and scholar; that of a Mexican American professor; that of a first-generation Mexican American student who began her postsecondary studies at a community college; and that of a Mexican American woman, parent, and member of a community along the United States–Mexico border.

In the past, my writing has followed a more traditional academic approach that typically includes the problem statement, a review of the existing literature on the subject matter, methodology, data collection, analysis, and implications for further research. It represented the broad base of scholarly training I received in my many years of studying educational psychology, counseling, and a multitude of theories at both the University of Texas at El Paso and New Mexico State University. It reflects my own theoretical frameworks, which evolved during my studies and are present in my dissertation and academic articles.

However, I find that it limits my "necessary subjectivity" (Ladson-Billings 1994, xi). I now integrate my voice in the research and writing process in order to enter the participants' worlds, teach them, and learn from them while utilizing a critical resilience framework. Thus this book is a blending of the knowledge gained from the academic world with my own personal experiences.

Each chapter describes ideas and principles that amplify what it means to be resilient. This introduction provides background information on community colleges and attempts to explain why I consider these institutions "gardens of possibility" where student resilience is cultivated. Chapters 1 and 2 provide the theoretical foundation of the protective and environmental factors based on current trends in psychology and describe teacher qualities that foster resilience. These chapters introduce a few students whose stories are good examples of the concepts presented. Chapter 3 describes how the professors' perspectives, philosophies, and teaching strategies and methods nurture resilience in students.

The next three chapters use narratives of Mexican Americans to portray how these students became stronger in the face of adversity by cultivating their larger purpose, experiencing validation, and exchanging social and cultural capital. Professors are featured throughout to illustrate that resilience is not just about survival but "is often endurance with direction" (Greitens 2015, 25). The stories show how these teachers guided the students and provided them with the necessary resources, knowledge, and support.

Mexican American families can also play an integral role in the growth, development, and success of their children through motivation and teachings, an area that is often overlooked and is therefore highlighted in these chapters. The final chapter summarizes how the dreams of community college students can become a reality through resilience. The appendix provides a summary description of the methodology that was used for this research.

STORIES AND EXAMPLES

All seven chapters include narrative examples that allow the reader to see how theory can be applied in real-life situations, by people from all walks of life. All the individuals described here experienced varying forms of barriers, challenges, obstacles, and frustrations, but managed to overcome them, learned their own unique lessons, and remained whole through the entire process. They each took their challenges and "twisted fibers of struggle into resilient yarn" (Campa 2013b, 79).

The stories come from the students and professors of El Paso Community College who provided inspiration as they strengthened their resilience. There are several compelling reasons to tell these stories. Narratives can help us understand our heroes' journeys, teach us about our own capacities for resilience, and show us how it can be fostered. Stories of struggle can demonstrate how knowledge from everyday life can serve as a tool and turn experiences into a breeding ground for survival strategies. Once we have an in-depth understanding of how to cultivate our own resilience, we can recognize it in others and help them transform their lives.

Sue Monk Kidd, famous for her essays and spiritual memoirs and well known for her *New York Times* best seller *The Secret Life of Bees*, once said that "stories have to be told or they die, and when they die, we can't remember who we are or why we're here." The stories in this book help us understand who we are and keep our experiences alive.

QUALITATIVE RESEARCH AS A JOURNEY

Qualitative research begins with the premise that reality can never be completely understood (Denzin and Lincoln 2000). Entering into the lived experiences of the participants as an observer, teacher, researcher, colleague, and friend and allowing them access into some of my worlds made me realize that this is what makes qualitative research both challenging and rewarding. I find myself going back and forth through my notes. Amazingly, every time I read and analyze their narratives, I gain new insights. These along with other experiences reinforce the notion that "qualitative research is endlessly creative and interpretive" (Denzin and Lincoln 2000, 23).

These journeys often continue long after the research is concluded. I still mentor some of the student participants and often collaborate with the professors who participated in the research. The care and *respeto* we have for each other is mutual and some of the students, who are now professionals in their own fields, continue to remain in contact with me. They eagerly follow my writing and inquire about my latest projects.

They always want to know how the process is coming along and, no matter how many obstacles I encounter, my response is always that "I'm working on it." It is their anticipation and interest in this qualitative research process and my desire to "lift as I climb" that motivates me to put pen to paper (Collins 2000; Knight 2004). I often share with my students the challenges and outright anxiety that can accompany research and writing. It is difficult, so I keep trudging along. Ralph Ellison (Jones 2002), famed novelist, critic, and scholar, once asked himself:

> So why do I write, torturing myself to put it down? Because in spite of myself I've learned some things. Without the possibility of action, all knowledge comes to one labeled "file and forget," and I can neither file nor forget. (471)

This book is only one step that my participants and I have taken together. It is part of a call for others to engage in the "community uplift" of Latino students (Villenas et al. 2006). Like many Latina feminists, I am passionate about this cause, and because the work of a qualitative researcher is never complete, I will remain fully engaged in this process. I will embrace what it means to be, in the words of one of my former students Amanda, a *mujer luchista* by moving forward and fighting back. This is the essence of resilience.

GARDENS OF POSSIBILITY

What makes community colleges unique and why are they such remarkable American institutions? Working with students has often been compared to gardening because of the parallels of nurturing an individual and bringing the flower out of the seed (Benard 2004). Great teachers, like experienced gardeners, understand that learning is an organic process. They cannot actually make something grow, but they can provide the seeds (our students) the type of environment that will promote their growth and development.

One teacher profiled by Gloria Ladson-Billings in *The Dreamkeepers: Successful Teachers of African American Children* observed that the students in her classroom were "God's little flowers." After a careful appraisal of her flowers, she concluded that "one might need a little sunlight, another a little fertilizer. Some might need a little pruning and some might need to roam free" (Ladson-Billings 1994, 89).

After many years of teaching, studying, and researching community colleges, I have come to the conclusion that they are truly gardens, gardens of possibility, in which seedlings flourish and are nurtured by women and men of the soil. Community colleges are gardens of possibility in which proper care and nurturing can produce vibrant flowers and magnificent plants. The professors I observed were great nurturers, tending their gardens, strengthening the resilience of their students, and allowing them to thrive. Few people realize the potential that these seedlings possess and how that potential can allow them to blossom into marvelous flowers.

Community colleges also embody our basic ideals of democracy and are often viewed as vehicles of access and opportunity (Rendón 1999; Baily and Morrest 2006). Twentieth-century liberal minister and activist Harry Emerson Fosdick (1878–1969), described by Dr. Martin Luther King Jr. as "one of the greatest preachers of this century," said that "democracy is based upon the conviction that there are extraordinary possibilities in ordinary people" (1958, 536).

Community colleges emerged and flourished in the era following the Second World War, when the United States saw itself as a world leader, fighting oppression and authority, protecting democracy, liberty, and equality. In 1947 a commission convened by President Harry Truman set a national goal of universal access to higher education so that all U.S. citizens could develop their abilities, contribute fully to the nation's growth, and achieve social mobility (Baily and Morrest 2006; Hutcheson 2007). An enlightened citizenry could then lead the world and extend these values and opportunities around the globe.

The Truman Commission recommended a system of tuition-free two-year colleges that would be within the reach of most Americans. Even though we never created a national system of tuition-free community colleges, the concept of equal access through "open doors" has become the primary institutional mission over the years. Equal access was designed to provide unlimited potential to almost any student interested in a college education. Community colleges now firmly embrace this idea and their open-door policies often provide ethnic and racial minorities, first-generation students, low-income students, and those who view community college as their last chance to realize their dreams with a great opportunity to pursue a postsecondary education (Rendón 1999).

Community colleges can also be seen as noble and humanitarian, offering people a fresh start, a place to correct errors or pursue missed opportunities of the past. At El Paso Community College, Professor Rose Galindo explained:

> The community college is about second chances. Many of the students who come to community college don't have a clear vision of what they want to do with their lives. Their options usually include getting a low-paying job, joining the military, or enrolling at a community college. They are scared to go to the university so they enroll at the community college. Our students come from very difficult circumstances and in class I sense their plea for help. They are telling me, that we [the community college] are their last hope.

These "second-chance" institutions have further transformed the landscape of American higher education by embracing students from very diverse backgrounds. Many of the students who rely greatly on these community colleges are underprepared, underrepresented, and underachieving. Often they are minority students who come from working-class backgrounds and are the first in their family to attend college. As Professor Galindo has witnessed, community colleges attract large numbers of students who are undecided, who literally do not know what to do, or who have nowhere else to go.

As community colleges grew, they soon discovered that many students were not ready for college-level work and a significant amount of remediation and developmental education was often necessary. At many institutions today, high percentages of course offerings are devoted to remedial education and almost half of the students entering two-year colleges are enrolled in these remedial courses (Complete College America 2012).

In recent decades, language instruction has become another factor, and community colleges have attracted a large number of immigrants and students who need to be more proficient in English. Along with language, they are interested in learning how to adapt to the customs of their new country (Grubb et al. 1999). These inclusive institutions of higher learning and their accommodations also appeal to students with disabilities, older college students, military men and women stationed around the world, and ethnic minorities.

Community colleges have embraced this new world with an "entrepreneurial spirit" or "willingness to accept new roles, an eagerness to expand into new markets" (Grubb et al. 1999, 7). Communities rely on their "community" colleges to meet the demands of new economies and a world that is always changing. These colleges' inclusiveness and democratic underpinnings, along with the willingness to serve their localities, has led to substantial growth in recent decades. They are no longer small neighborhood substitutes for universities, but instead have become large, prominent institutions of higher education (Schuetz 2002).

Practical considerations have added to this growth as well. For many years, community colleges focused on vocational training; however, a major shift took place toward the end of the twentieth century. Academic transfer courses became a larger part of their mission, and universities often welcomed the growth of community college remedial courses and language programs as gateways to a four-year institution.

Community colleges usually serve a large metropolitan population and cater to commuter students. They were not expected to provide the full, traditional college experience. As bare-bones facilities without the tremendous expenses of research institutions, community colleges became an economical way to educate a large portion of the population. Although it was never really the intention, the growth of academic transfer classes at community colleges attracted more and more traditional freshmen and sophomore students, drawn by the cost savings and convenient locations.

University-bound students were encouraged to begin their studies at community colleges. Articulation agreements and core curriculum offerings legitimized the process. Dual credit and early college arrangements with local school districts added to the growth. Enrollment numbers soared throughout the nation.

BACKGROUND AND PURPOSE

El Paso Community College followed these national and regional trends. The participants in this study attended an institution where the student body is approximately 85 percent Latino (EPCC 2010). El Paso Community College is spread over five campuses and with more than thirty thousand credit students and ten thousand continuing education students, it is one of the fastest growing community colleges in the country (EPCC 2011).

In 2013 El Paso Community College was cited as having the largest Latino faculty and having awarded the largest number of associate degrees to Latinos among all community colleges in the nation (Cooper 2013). The college serves El Paso, Texas, and its Mexican counterpart Ciudad Juárez, Chihuahua, located on the international border just across the Rio Grande. During the past fifty years, this area has been an economically disadvantaged but rapidly growing region of the country.

El Paso Community College has a large non-English-speaking population that often begins by studying English as a Second Language. Many of these students move through several levels of the program and then seek employment in the El Paso area. Others continue by enrolling in El Paso Community College's vocational programs. Some students, after completing the ESL program, enter academic credit classes conducted in English, which transfer to area universities. By the 2020s, El Paso Community College is expecting enrollment of more than forty thousand students.

WHY DO LATINOS CHOOSE COMMUNITY COLLEGES?

Latinos are drawn to community colleges in particularly large numbers. Part of the explanation lies in the demographic trends of the late twentieth century. The "Sunbelt" states grew dramatically and attracted people from declining regions in the northeast. The new centers of population and economic growth, California, Texas, and Florida, were states that also had rapidly growing Latino populations. Through immigration, migration, and traditionally higher fertility rates, the Latino population swelled and concentrated in large urban areas where community colleges were already growing.

While traditional four-year colleges and university centers continued to expand, they never quite matched the growth at community colleges. This growth put pressure on educational institutions as larger and larger segments of the population attended community colleges. Community colleges were accessible, often with branch campuses spread throughout the metropolitan area. They were also comparatively a lot less expensive.

Community colleges expanded and offered more courses that would transfer to area four-year institutions. They soon developed a full range of freshman and sophomore courses, articulation agreements with local and regional institutions, and "core" curriculums that allowed full blocks of classes to be easily moved to degree programs and four-year colleges. Some promoted themselves as a way to ease into academic studies, become accustomed to the college culture, and polish up any needed skills before making the transition. They called themselves the "best place to start." Kurlaender (2006) used logistic regression analyses to explore the factors that influence Latinos' high rates of enrollment and found that when compared to other racial minority groups with similar academic preparation and socioeconomic status, Latinos consistently choose community colleges over universities.

Several factors influenced the decision, and recent studies have argued that the picture is quite complex (Schuetz 2002; Vaughn 2005). In a qualitative study of community college students, Somers, Haines, and Keene (2006) found that their decision to pursue an education at these institutions came as a result of financial, educational, and personal setbacks. Some of the reasons cited were the one-on-one attention available, increased faculty contact, the willingness of faculty to help with their studies, the extensive learning support services, and the "small school experiences" made possible by having fewer students in each class (Somers et al. 2006).

Kurlaender (2006) concluded that among Latinos, race, more than academic achievement or socioeconomic status, influenced the decision to enroll in community colleges. He suggests that the proximity of a community college to their homes might be an important factor in influencing their choice. Fry (2002) found a similar pattern and reported that close ties of Latinos to their family and community appear to contribute to their exceptionally high rates of enrollment in community colleges.

The open-door admission policy, or open enrollment at these institutions, which only requires students to have a high school diploma or something equivalent, also attracts many Latinos (Krogstad and Fry 2015). This may be beneficial for those who are unprepared for college. Because Latino students are more likely to attend college on a part-time basis, the flexibility of an institution is also an important factor (Fry 2002). Unlike most universities, community colleges offer degree programs and class schedules that accommodate part-time students.

MY JOURNEY

I faced many challenges in my early life. My challenges, and often brutal realities, were similar to the lives of many El Paso Community College students. I was born and raised in poverty in a Mexican *colonia* overlooking El Paso, Texas. My mother and I lived in a small, meager dwelling with a large extended family of dear people who lacked even the most basic education and training. We struggled through life, surviving each day, and endured long periods of time when there was little work or food. We were also victims of criminal violence. Our lives were chaotic and confusing, a gloomy existence with little hope. While we were resourceful, there was no critical thinking or long-range planning involved in our day-to-day lives.

We certainly worked hard. I fondly recall the image of my grandmother. She had two neatly tied Indian braids of an unnatural blue-black color, dyed to cover her premature white hair. She had a small, frail appearance but was steady and a very diligent worker. She had the most beautiful dark brown face, with hundreds of wrinkles caused by the sun, sixty years of chain smoking, and a harsh, tragic life. Those wrinkles earned my grandmother a deep level of respect, love, and admiration from her large extended family of eight children and twelve grandchildren.

When I was a young girl, this family matriarch regularly crossed the border between Ciudad Juárez and El Paso, cleaning houses and working at odd jobs to earn a few dollars to keep the family going. The homes she worked in were modest; they often hired her out of pity and paid her with a sack of beans or potatoes. As the day ended, "La Llorona" dutifully dragged the sacks across the bridge to bring back to our small home in the colonia above Ciudad Juárez.

All through the time I was growing up, my grandmother kept the family going despite unbelievable hardships and tragedies. She was the rock that the entire family relied on. Many years went by, and a few of us escaped the colonia and found better lives elsewhere. She continued to trudge along, overseeing the growing family and always working hard.

Each day was a struggle to survive. When my mother was a small child, she was sent out into the neighborhood with an old metal bucket, knocking on doors and asking for food. My grandmother chose her for this important task because she was the youngest and the cutest among the children, and so the most likely to convince a neighbor to share some of whatever little they had. Sometimes she was gone all day, wandering through the hillsides of the poor, sometimes dangerous shantytown, gathering whatever she could to help the family out.

On a good day, she would return with some rice or scraps of tortilla, enough for her brothers and sister to have something to eat that evening. Surrounded by families with similar problems and roaming the streets at a very young age, my mother sought comfort among other desperate children. At the age of thirteen, this child became pregnant, and a few months later, I was born. By doing so, she brought one more hungry mouth to feed into the household.

As a small child, I struggled but was often unaware of the depth of suffering and deprivation we endured. Throughout the day I carried buckets of water from the local well to the house, I ran errands and, at times, I felt privileged to run our *tiendita* or modest "store," a small table and awning where we sold sodas and candy to the neighbors, one of our many entrepreneurial ventures that never quite got off the ground.

At that time in the 1970s, Ciudad Juárez was growing rapidly and more people were crossing the river, not just to earn a few dollars, but to seek a much better life. After we crossed, we found that opportunities were still limited for people like my mother, and she soon found out that abundant poverty and despair existed in the land of opportunity. She entered into another doomed relationship and married a physically and psychologically abusive man who made her life miserable and often terrorized her children. She endured twelve years of severe abuse and was finally saved when my stepfather, lost in one of his cycles of alcohol and drugs, surrounded by a cohort of enablers, drowned in a common public swimming pool.

By that time, our household had grown. I had two small sisters to look after while my mother worked at a local factory. Life became even more difficult after my stepfather's death. Because my mother and I were not of Native American descent, we were banished from the Tigua Indian Reservation. The little security we had gained suddenly vanished.

I asked myself how we could break out of this miserable life, how we could achieve all that we saw around us. If I could move forward, I could lead the way and ultimately help my family follow the same path. I began to understand the power of education and was driven to succeed. I was able to break out of the cycle and make use of entirely new resources and opportunities.

By the time I was eighteen, I had graduated from an El Paso high school and had become a citizen of the United States. But my skills were limited and traditional university studies were beyond my reach. I enrolled at El Paso Community College and began a long process of developing basic skills, setting goals, and planning a career. My experiences were tremendous. Friendly, patient teachers helped me explore new areas and polish my skills. High standards allowed me to prepare for university studies. I was not aware of it at the time, but I was actually the first Hispanic female to attend El Paso Community College after high school, build my skills for university studies, transfer to the University of Texas at El Paso, go on to earn a doctorate at New Mexico State University, and become a full-tenured professor at El Paso Community College.

Throughout these opportunities and challenges, I had built a reasonable degree of social competence; I became autonomous, set goals, made plans, and achieved many of my dreams. Through my research and writing, I had the honor of meeting and studying with countless individuals who had faced similar challenges in their lives and had overcome obstacles of all kinds to eventually become successful, productive students and teachers.

Many community college students do not have a clear strategy to get to the next step in life or to establish and pursue a goal. Many of the professors we will meet in the coming chapters helped students develop an overall plan to work toward life goals. My first real step toward problem solving and autonomy was when I entered El Paso Community College and began to truly understand how educational goals can help students focus and ultimately empower them. I saw this process again and again as I observed people who built resilience, thrived in the academic world, and broke intergenerational cycles of poverty. But at the time, college students often had to seek help on their own, use trial and error, or find an individual counselor or teacher who could guide them along and help them plan. Something was missing.

THE FIRST-YEAR EXPERIENCE

Studies have shown that the first year of college is critical for students to succeed. The first year "is especially significant for certain populations: students of color, nontraditional students, first-generation college students, low-income students, under-prepared students, and those for whom English is a second language" (Anderson 2004, 77). Community college students are often at risk and are particularly susceptible to becoming discouraged, drop-ping out of or failing classes, not returning the following semester, and never graduating.

Overall, community colleges have instituted a variety of programs and support services to promote success among entering college students. One of these programs is the first-year experience course, also referred to as the freshman experience, learning frameworks, and student success (Barefoot and Fidler 1996; Jalomo and Rendón 2004; O'Gara et al. 2008). These classes attempt to identify problems early, provide guidance and inspiration, and put students on the right path to success.

The organization and content varies among institutions, but the overall goal of these courses is very similar. They are aimed at new students, prefer-ably those in their first semester, and are designed to enhance the overall college experience (Jalomo and Rendón 2004). They offer students informa-tion about campus resources, assistance in academic and career planning, establishing relationships with peers, staff, and faculty members, and en-hancing study habits and other personal skills (Barefoot and Fidler 1996; O'Gara et al. 2008; Stovall 2000).

The overarching task of this course is to provide students from diverse backgrounds a college experience that is meaningful and is rich enough to help them survive and thrive in postsecondary education. The first-year expe-rience course was created with these new freshman students in mind. Materi-als and the curriculum for the first-year experience courses help students reevaluate their lives, perform better in college classes, and set new goals for the future.

Sharon K. Ferrett, author of the widely used textbook *Peak Performance: Success in College and Beyond*, argues that peak performers excel "because they know they possess the personal power to produce results and find pas-sion in what they contribute to life" (2015, 2). Studies have found that stu-dents, especially minority students, who participate in a first-year experience course generally improve their academic performance (Barefoot and Gardner 1993; O'Gara et al. 2008; Stovall 2000). In other words, these classes vali-date students and help them build resilience.

Education 1300 is El Paso Community College's first-year experience course. Its roots are in the national movement that dates back to the 1980s, when even at the most prestigious universities, professors and support staff realized that students often needed help in the transition. Community col-leges found these courses to be particularly useful for nontraditional students and students of color. The courses were soon found to help validate student experiences, build a bridge to traditional academic work, and allow students to foster resilience.

Education 1300 builds basic skills and broadens a student's thoughts and perspectives. Primary college skills, such as note taking, time management, and test taking, are essential in most fields of study, and so they are important components of the curriculum. In addition, students work with library resources, technology, communications, research projects, and writing. A lot more importantly, Education 1300 helps students understand new ideas and concepts, allowing them to closely examine their own lives and begin a journey of personal and career development.

Students are asked to integrate and apply learning, motivation, and metacognitive theories in order to foster academic success. Counseling, psychology, career exploration, and critical thinking are all parts of the foundation of the course. Education 1300 encourages students to apply various learning paradigms in order to make behavioral changes that will have a positive impact on their studies and help redefine their role in society.

At "second-chance" institutions such as El Paso Community College, in our gardens of possibility, this process is extremely important. I found that the college not only attracts students from diverse backgrounds and those who are at the margins, but also draws professors with the intellectual, emotional, and spiritual fabric necessary to cultivate the resilience of these students. In fact, it was fairly easy to find professors who were just as persistent, courageous, and resilient as the students they teach. Time and again, some of the same names appeared—teachers that our students found to be particularly effective.

Community colleges are known for attracting individuals with a deep desire to teach. These teachers have often gone through an inquiry process and have developed a larger purpose, one of which is helping students transform their lives. When reflecting on teaching, we often focus on which subjects are taught, what methods should be used, and how classes are to be structured.

But Parker J. Palmer believes that those interested in education frequently fail to ask themselves one central question: "Who is the self that teaches?" He argues that teaching cannot be reduced to simply intellect, the subject being taught, or techniques because the students and subjects we teach "are as large and complex as life" (1998, 2).

> If the students and subjects accounted for all the complexities of teaching, our standard ways of coping would do—keep up with our fields as best we can and learn enough techniques to stay ahead of the student psyche. But there is another reason for these complexities: We teach who we are.

The resilient professors in this study are very much aware that they "teach who they are." During classroom observations, I often felt excited, inspired, and almost mesmerized by what I was seeing. I struggled with how these classroom experiences, which were intriguing, deeply engaging, and enchanting at times, could ever be put into words.

I once hiked a medieval trade route in northern Italy known as the Cinque Terre, a trek through a string of five ancient villages on the Italian Riviera on a rugged, rocky shoreline with incredibly stunning panoramic views of the sea. I was frustrated with the futility of attempting to record such an incredible vista and aura. I knew that no written description or photograph could ever depict the majestic blue ocean, the picturesque seascape, or the multicolored flora in a meaningful way. How can one capture such a profound experience?

I was often frustrated in the same way after observing my colleagues' classrooms. I felt privileged to visit the spaces these teachers had created and was moved by the connections, interactions, and deep relationships they often had with their students. These professors were humble, open, and respectful of their students. They knew all their students' names, their idiosyncrasies, their likes and dislikes, and their strengths and weaknesses. Respecting their students meant honoring their needs. The experience of being immersed in their worlds was similar to that of hiking in the Cinque Terre. It was unique, complex, powerful, and I panicked when I began to think about how I would capture such a profound experience and describe it to others.

DRAMA IN THE GARDEN

Meet Lisa McNiel, professor of Speech and Drama. She is a tall, slender, blue-eyed, blonde theater coordinator who directs cutting-edge plays at El Paso Community College. Her confident and dramatic flair commands attention and respect from her audience. This popular professor is an actress at heart and is known for using the classroom as a stage for acting and role-playing psychodramas and other performances. Students describe her as "unpredictable, spontaneous, enthusiastic, and funny." They like Professor McNiel's ability to "inspire confidence in them." When I heard comments such as "I am terrified of speaking in public but Ms. McNiel taught me how to relax and have fun while delivering speeches," I had to witness this with my own eyes!

I quickly learned that Professor McNiel borrows ideas and techniques from the works of Jung, Campbell, Freud, and other pioneers in psychology. She does this in order to help students overcome interpersonal and inter-psychic barriers to master successful public speaking. McNiel explained that "obstacles often manifest themselves in the form of anxiety, fear, inferiority, or perfectionism when delivering speeches." Many students of college-going age are going through transitional stages of development and suffer from anxiety not only in the classroom, but also in their everyday lives.

In class, McNiel teaches students about interpersonal communication. She discusses the inner critic or private audience, how it is created, and the power it has in hindering our self-esteem and public speaking abilities. She explains that we are not born with negative messages; these come from interactions with other people. McNiel introduces Fritz Perls's "Gestalt Empty Chair" technique, an interactive therapeutic tool that involves imagining someone who is sitting in the chair. The empty chair helps us engage with our thoughts, feelings, and behaviors in order to address some of the interpsychic blocks that hold us back.

McNiel reaches to a nearby table that is covered in props. She picks up a blue baseball cap with one hand and twists and pushes her silky, shiny blonde hair into a ball with the other. Her facial expressions and voice turn masculine as soon as the cap is placed on her head. She becomes her ex-husband, telling Lisa "you have no realistic way of achieving your dreams" after she shares her future aspirations of working on her master's degree and eventually a doctorate in Communications. McNiel then removes the baseball cap, switches to the other chair, and acts out the disintegrated part of herself that "believes her ex-husband is right" and voices in a soft and defeated way "Yeap! I don't have the skills and talents required."

After she stands up from the chair, McNiel explains that these comments, along with inner dialogue, generated the self-doubt that led her to "shortchange herself." The exchange is authentic and makes her seem vulnerable in the eyes of her students.

Then McNiel asks for volunteers. Surprisingly, many of the students raise their hands and are eager to go to the front of the class and sit next to an empty chair. Five are selected and are asked to think of a person who conveyed negative messages and to visualize them sitting in the chair. Using psychodrama techniques, such as role-reversal and mirroring, they are guided through the past experience in order to bring to the surface underlying beliefs. The class becomes enraptured and enthralled in the drama. The audience silently watches as Margarita, a young Hispanic female, tells the following story:

> When I was in high school my counselor discouraged me from going to college. Even though she never told me directly that I did not have what it takes to go to college she ignored me and never did anything to help me. Her actions made me doubt myself and led me to believe I had a learning disability.

McNiel reaches across to the prop table and puts on her gold-colored Captain Kirk shirt and "bounces" her ex-husband out of her audience. Margarita and the other volunteers are asked to tap into their true self, "bounce those people out of their audience," and replace them with supportive, loving people who will reject negative beliefs and help to restore their confidence.

The class was stunned by the exchange, locked in an experience in which they were almost born again. Later I thought, "Wow, where was Professor

McNiel when I attended El Paso Community College?" Then I realized that these fabulous teaching experiences were some of the best kept secrets in higher education; obscure, hidden, quietly thriving in the garden. Perhaps even more significant was the realization that such experiences were not commonly acknowledged, and in many case, were ignored in community colleges.

The trend in secondary education has been to downplay the individual teacher and focus on curriculum and outcomes. Public schools view them as facilitators rather than creative motivators. They are to be trained rather than educated and their role has become one of simply guiding students through scheduled materials prepared by experts, with curriculum and assessment materials that have been created by agencies and commercial vendors. This same trend is seeping into community colleges.

Fortunately, I was delighted to find that our resilient faculty members are truly teachers. Perhaps they are seldom noticed, but they are well-educated, motivated, lifelong learners who practice a craft. Their resilience and their deep connection to their disciplines and their students set them apart. Community colleges are under the same pressures to conform; however, many professors have continued to follow their own unique paths and use creative, inspiring methods to develop resilience in their students. While the academic world around them revs up with standardization and technology, they remain busy, tending the garden. Perhaps they have a better chance of surviving and thriving if they remain invisible.

HONORED BUT INVISIBLE

Community colleges are often overwhelmed with too many purposes, a lack of funding, and a wide range of pedagogical issues. They are overlooked, misunderstood, and poorly represented in the literature. The general public knows little about them, and they are often cited for their technical or vocational programs, even though the overwhelming majority of students are enrolled in academic courses. Community colleges hover somewhere in between, designed to be a bridge between the public school system and universities. Many community colleges have adopted broad, fuzzy mission statements dedicating their institutions to "improvement" or "workforce development." Some studies have concluded that they are almost "invisible," unseen and unknown.

In *Honored but Invisible*, Grubb and his associates describe a common problem at open-admissions institutions, which the faculty have been aware of all along: teaching and learning are often ignored while the debate focuses on "conflicts over *means*—funding, political control, personnel policies, the allocation of space and equipment" (1999, 1). Too often, the administrators' "political and managerial roles swamp their roles as educational leaders" (1999, 1).

It may not be entirely their fault. The literature on community colleges is quite limited and has a narrowed focus. Most community colleges do not exist in academic literature, and when they do, they are often studied by university researchers who have not actually worked at a community college or have had much contact with its faculty or students. Most studies focus on basic managerial issues of enrollment, articulation, retention, and curriculum. Although there are a few high-quality journals dedicated to studying these institutions, the emphasis is often the same.

Creative teaching or broad pedagogical issues are seldom featured. Part of the problem is that community college faculty members are seldom encouraged to study or publicize their work on students. Administrators often see research and publication, even when it directly applies to the classroom, as a distraction and something that diminishes quality teaching or commitment to the institution.

Very little is known about what happens in the classrooms of these important institutions. While universities will often encourage research in their own classrooms or local school districts, few professors conduct studies in community colleges. It appears that most people assume that whatever works in a high school or university will work in a community college.

Community colleges are also invisible to the students who attend them. These students are almost always commuters who spend a few hours a day on campus and then return to their busy everyday lives. The vast majority do not complete associate degrees. Large attrition rates add to the problem. Many students take a class or two and never return. They have little connection to the college and rarely participate in campus life, activities, clubs, or public events. Few community colleges have active alumni associations or strong connections to the broader communities they serve.

The general public knows little about their local community colleges. Athletic activities draw small crowds and are overshadowed by university sports. Community college architecture and landscape seldom draw visitors to the campus. Unlike traditional universities' complexes or idyllic campus settings, few people spend a leisurely afternoon strolling through the local community college. They are just there, off the side of the road, like any number of office complexes or strip malls along the highway.

But invisibility can also be an asset. Being out of the spotlight has sometimes allowed community college faculty to thrive, innovate, and experiment. These gardens of possibility are invisible because people do not know about the miracles and transformations that happen in these spaces every day. They have not witnessed time and time again how individuals twist fibers of struggle into resilient yarn and improve their lives and those of their loved ones. Listening to students and professors talk about their heroic journeys of struggle and survival inspired me to write these stories down on paper so that others could learn from them as much as I have.

Chapter One

Resilience and Personal Protective Factors

Stories about those who triumph in the face of adversity have captivated the hearts and minds of people for centuries. They have compelled developmental scientists and researchers to study resilience and learn how people transcend difficult or tragic circumstances and move on with their lives. In the 1970s a small cohort of psychologists, led by doctors Emmy E. Werner and Ruth S. Smith, set out to examine this elusive idea of resilience or "how individuals overcome overwhelming odds to become stronger." Werner's path-breaking, lifelong works led future scholars to revere her as the "mother" of resilience studies (Snyder and Lopez 2007, 103).

Even though early research focuses mostly on children, over time others have studied how adults, who experience severe hardship, manage to achieve healthy development, academic success, and normal, productive lives (Rutter 1987; Wolin and Wolin 1993). Resilience studies broadened their horizons and began to examine other cases, such as victims of physical and mental abuse, refugees, Holocaust survivors, victims of crime, and those facing severe illnesses.

MATTIE: A MODEL OF RESILIENCE

In the 1990s Mattie J. T. Stepanek became one of the most celebrated examples cited by psychologists for his incredible strength and perseverance and recognized around the world as an exemplary model of resilience. In *Messenger*, Mattie's mother Jeni Stepanek (2009) tells the story of her courageous son, born with a rare form of muscular dystrophy, who gained international acclaim through his poetry, compassion, and optimism. He inspired millions around the world with his peacemaking efforts, speeches, and writings. Even though Mattie had to endure many surgeries, blood transfusions, and extensive medical treatments, cope with his mother's disability, and grieve the loss of his three older siblings, he transcended his dire medical struggles and turned them into a message of peace and hope.

Mattie used the word "heartsong" to describe a person's inner self, and at the age of three began composing poems and short stories that embellished the concept. Adversity made him thrive and psychologists noted that this miracle child "became more prolific as the neuromuscular disease he battled became more difficult to manage" (Snyder and Lopez 2007, 103). Mattie dealt with many family tragedies, his ailing mother, and his constant medical treatments, but never gave up.

He encouraged people to "play after every storm!" Oprah Winfrey welcomed this child as a "big soul in a little boy's body" and former president Jimmy Carter, along with millions of people around the world, celebrated Mattie until his death at the age of thirteen.

How can Mattie's incredible stamina and perseverance against all odds be understood? What contributed to this extraordinary example of human resilience? Rather than succumbing to the tragedy, he became skilled at communicating messages of hope, empathy, and compassion. Mattie, like many people, had factors that protected him from such hopeless conditions and helped build his resilience. These factors strengthened him physically, emotionally, and spiritually, while inspiring others.

THE RESILIENCE FRAMEWORK

Few people will ever face the challenges that Mattie was forced to endure and develop such persistent, driven optimism. But everyone has elements of resilience that can be built upon. Resilience is not one specific set of traits in an individual. It is a dynamic process that involves an interaction among risk, vulnerability, and protective factors that over time help to modify the effects of a difficult life event (Reyes and Elias 2011).

A common misconception is that the "resilient journey" must involve great loss and dramatic recovery, but Dr. Erik Morales notes that personal challenges are "individual and relative" and sometimes rather minor (2013, 15). Each person faces their own day-to-day crises and obstacles, and how they react determines their resilience.

The study of resilience is relatively new. For most of the twentieth century, psychologists, psychiatrists, and counselors have focused their research and practices on human problems primarily, looking at disease, maladjustment, and symptoms. Wolin and Wolin (1993) call this the "damage model," a view that focuses on whatever is wrong with an individual. In the field of education, this is known as the "deficit model." Once what is "wrong" has been understood, a treatment can be prescribed.

The *Diagnostic and Statistical Manual of Mental Disorders* (DSM), published by the American Psychiatric Association, is a handbook that details the criteria and symptom descriptions used by professionals to diagnose mental disorders. It currently contains almost one thousand densely written pages that describe in great detail the maladies that plague the lives of the mentally ill. It strongly supports this medical model and continues to influence people's understanding of psychological wellness.

Toward the late twentieth century, a new field of study emerged. Rather than looking at what is "wrong" in an individual with a problem, resilience researchers turned their focus to how an individual confronts a problem; in other words, what is "right" with that individual, and how they use this to overcome a crisis or obstacle, how people "find healthy ways to integrate" adverse "experiences into their lives" (Greitens 2015, 23). Resilience studies look at strengths; how they are acquired, developed, and are used to face adversity.

Resilience is therefore a new paradigm, a shift in thinking, or a new way of seeing the world. It is a paradigm "conditioned by inborn temperament, upbringing, family, friends, colleagues, schooling and work environment" (Wolin and Wolin 2007, 124). The Wolins suggest that traumas and adversity can be seen as "challenges" rather than "damages" without discounting human pain and suffering (2007, 129). In the meantime, a new field of "positive" psychology emerged. Dr. Martin E. P. Seligman, president of the American Psychological Association in the late 1990s, led the efforts to define this field as one that focuses on promoting the wellness rather than focusing on the illness of individuals.

Positive psychologists, using the theory of humanism, brought the concept of resilience into their work (Csikszentmihalyi 1996; Seligman 1998). Some have suggested that this new paradigm needs to be studied more fully such that eventually it becomes an integral part of the *Diagnostic and Statistical Manual* in order to gain a more complete understanding of people (Blundo 2006; Saleebey 2006). These researchers found that almost everyone has the ability to be resilient. Eventually everyone experiences loss, death and separation, and personal and physical challenges during their lives. How someone deals with these adversities can reveal their levels of resilience. Sometimes a person faces a relatively minor crisis and is almost destroyed by the ordeal. In other cases, people can experience severe adversity but are able to bounce back in some way and move on with their lives.

PERSONAL PROTECTIVE FACTORS

In the 1990s Bonnie Benard summarized four basic characteristics of resilience and described them as protective factors. These are essentially internal attributes, personal strengths, manifestations, and attitudes that have been found to help resilient individuals, such as Mattie Stepanek, the students and professors at El Paso Community College, and anyone experiencing personal struggles, deal with difficult situations. Resilient individuals draw on four basic factors: social competence, problem solving, a sense of autonomy, and a larger sense of purpose (Benard 1993, 2004).

These factors appear to "transcend ethnicity, culture, gender, geography, and time" (cited in Benard 2004, 13, from Werner and Smith 1992, 2001). They can be developed and cultivated over time and taught in a way that helps people with very low levels of resilience overcome adversity. Not every person exhibits all of these factors, but they can each contribute to the overall development of the individual. As people successfully build solid foundations of resilience, they can move further and become altruistic, mindful, and achieve high levels of happiness and fulfillment.

Social Competence

Basic social competence is an important personal protective factor. Benard describes it as the "characteristics, skills, and attitudes essential to forming relationships and positive attachments"; in other words, the ability to communicate with and be responsive to people (Benard 2004, 14). Social competency can be very basic, simply connecting to a person and receiving a positive response. Through this connection, an individual can build communication skills and cultivate relationships. Social competency can create opportunities to work with peers, build social networks, seek out mentors, and eventually obtain social and cultural capital.

Angel is a twenty-nine-year-old bilingual Mexican American male. When he was a child, Angel's father abandoned his family, leaving them to struggle for many years. His mother migrated to the United States as an undocumented worker at a young age. She had little education and supported herself and Angel by holding several low-paying, manual labor jobs.

Today he comes across as serious, friendly, and inquisitive, but this was not always the case. His educational experiences as a child were good. Angel enjoyed school and developed interests in science and music. He had a special interest in geology and every time he came across a rock, he would pick it up, look at it, and wonder where it came from or how it was created. But by middle school, things began to change. He was bored with his studies and spent more time with a growing circle of friends who cared little for school or its formalities. He had minimal connections with his teachers and began avoiding extracurricular activities. Angel had moved into "the wrong crowd," hanging out and partying rather than pursuing his studies or socializing with successful students.

While middle school can often be a time when students rebel or disconnect, in Angel's case it had become a long-term process of decline. Each year he drifted further away from his studies. But he still had a lingering interest in geology. The problem was that in his social circles, being a "geek was not cool," and no one was particularly interested in science or nature. After a while, he stopped talking about rocks and started focusing on "fitting in." By high school, he had lost whatever knowledge he had gained of geology, math, or music. His grades went further downhill and he attended fewer and fewer classes. Eventually Angel dropped out of high school.

After a while, he returned and was sent to an alternative high school, a place where students were put in self-paced tutorial programs to master the most basic skills. The assignments were dull and tedious, and Angel was once again discouraged. He was unable to connect with the faculty or the counselors and eventually left the program. At that point, Angel became just another statistic: a poor, Hispanic male dropout with few skills and a very limited future. Following this failure, he started working in a series of low-paying jobs as a laborer.

However, he never entirely gave up and eventually earned a high school equivalency certificate or GED and went on to attend community college. But the years of poor performance in middle school and high school caught up with him once again, and he was placed in a series of remedial classes. Bored and discouraged, he left community college as well. Angel got married at twenty-two and worked as a truck driver. He drove an 80,000-pound semi-trailer truck all over the country.

He was glad to work that job and needed the money to support his family, but for the first time he experienced a sense of anxiety and fear. Schedules and deadlines made truck driving difficult, and maneuvering the huge vehicle "was a lot of responsibility" because he had "to take other people's lives into consideration," not just his own. He drove to New York City in 2001, after the September 11 attacks. He passed through Louisiana shortly after Hurricane Katrina had hit New Orleans in 2005. Spending time in other parts of the country and interacting with many different types of people broadened his perspectives.

Driving for many hours along dark roads or brightly lit interstate highways brought loneliness, but also the opportunity to think and reflect on his early life experiences and his future. He thought about many of the poor decisions he had made. He missed his family and was becoming uncomfortable with life on the road.

Angel never fully lost his interest in geology, and occasionally it would jolt him back to reality. In one interview, he explained how the transition took place:

Interviewer: I saw a *molcajete* the other day and I thought about you. The round piece of black rock that is used to grind chile. I wonder what type of rock it is made of?

Angel: Is that what it is called? I know it is an extrusive rock because of the way it is shaped and the air bubbles. It is vesicular because anything that has air bubbles is vesicular. It is extrusive because it comes out of the earth. When it's extrusive it is from within the earth and pushed out. I didn't know why but that's what I do when I look at rocks. Ever since I was little I would name the rocks. Then I would tell my friends and they would say, "That's what?" I would say never mind, man. They would say, "It's just a rock, dude." I would say, "It's more than just a rock."

The interest in earth science remained within him, always there just under the surface.

Women have always been a very powerful influence in Angel's life. His grandmother was abandoned and left to raise ten children on her own. His father left his mother as well, and she struggled to support the family. Angel's mother had always known that he had potential and urged him to return to school. Ten years had passed and Angel now had a one-year-old son, Carlitos. His sister, who had a decent paying job and was able to "lift as she climbed," allowed him and his family to live in her house. As Angel matured, he learned respect and responsibility from these women. After many hours of reflecting about his future and that of his wife, Angel decided to return to West Texas and enroll in El Paso Community College. This time, with a bit of maturity and experience, he became more resilient.

He studied geology with Professor Sulaiman Abushagur, who rekindled his interest and enthusiasm for learning and helped him develop the social competency that he needed to connect with others and become a more successful student. He found Dr. Abushagur to be a "great teacher who inspired and pushed him to new limits," someone who always led him just a bit further and opened up new worlds. Angel admired how Dr. Abushagur was able to explain dense scientific concepts in geology in simple enough terms for students to understand while still maintaining their complexity and meaning.

Angel also found that his professor had a relaxed, fun, and entertaining style that made the class more enjoyable. He noticed that his teacher was both fun and funny. Angel began to see Dr. Abushagur as his role model, someone who represented what Angel wanted to be when he entered the academic and professional world. In turn, his professor was impressed by his friendly personality, sense of humor, and hard-working nature. He saw Angel open up and become more engaged with the students and teachers.

Eventually, Angel helped with geological tours to areas around EPCC's Transmountain Campus on the edge of Franklin Mountains State Park. He attended art shows, movies, cultural festivals, and many other college activities. This new social competency led Dr. Abushagur to recommend him for a tutoring position in the science lab where he could help other students learn about geology. Angel now sees the nerdy, "geek" image as cool and wants to pursue a career in science, hoping someday to become a geology professor. He hopes this will inspire his son and the future generations in his family. At El Paso Community College, Angel had developed a social competency that led him to new opportunities in his studies and helped him become more resilient.

Throughout this book, there are many examples of how basic social competency has led students to greater academic success and achievement. Social competency can begin with a simple, basic, positive relationship that can then play a powerful role in building resilience. Children who succeed against incredible odds often have at least one close personal connection with a caregiver or another adult (Belsky 2013; Werner and Smith 1992). Jeni Stepanek, Mattie's mother, confined to a wheelchair with the same neuro-muscular condition as Mattie, was his greatest strength. She was a strongly committed and impassioned parent who made Mattie's life a good experience while facing her own mortality (Stepanek 2009).

Jeni surrounded Mattie with a social support system of people who loved him deeply. They were not biologically his family, but they became dear, supportive friends of Mattie and often went far beyond what a typical family would do to nurture Jeni and Mattie. This web of personal relationships created an environment in which Mattie was at ease and could flourish. His social competency bloomed, and he became comfortable with all types of people.

Many of the community college students described here made basic social connections that allowed them to build their resilience and helped them succeed academically. Some developed long-term connections and acquired mentors and social and cultural capital as a result of these relationships.

Social competency can also produce empathy, the ability to understand other people's feelings and perspectives. Being able to read other people's feelings from nonverbal clues can make a person more outgoing, popular, and in some cases more well-liked in the classroom. Empathy can move one to respond to others' needs in unselfish ways. It involves mirroring other people's emotions and often engenders a tenderheartedness toward another person (Snyder and Lopez 2007). Many of the students and faculty discussed in this book have developed high levels of empathy, especially the professors who cultivate close relationships with their students. Empathy is considered a hallmark of resilience (Werner and Smith 1992).

Empathy can also lead to forgiveness, which is beneficial to a person's overall psychological well-being (Snyder and Lopez 2007). Forgiveness allows people to heal and move on with their lives. It does not mean that they condone, pardon, or excuse the person who causes harm. Nor does it require feelings of love toward the transgressor or the reestablishment of a relationship with the transgressor (Thompson et al. 2005).

Forgiveness is something kind that people do for themselves when they release negative associations and no longer allow an event or person to dominate their lives. Empirical research shows that holding on to anger causes harm in both physical and psychological ways. In some cases, people need to forgive themselves, to stop questioning their decisions or the mistakes they had made earlier in life so they can release their anger and guilt. Forgiveness can enhance resilience and produces a healthier, happier person (Lyubomirsky 2007). Dr. Fred Luskin (2003) dedicated his life to research on forgiveness, and one of his principal ideas is that at the heart of forgiveness are the issues of gratitude and compassion.

If gratitude and real thankfulness are practiced on a daily basis, an internal alignment can be experienced that leaves no room for wanting to harm someone else. Luskin suggests that people look beyond their own problems to ask "Why am I so wrapped in my own suffering?" If a person offers a bit more kindness than they receive, they will be healthier, happier, and more resilient. Many of the students and professors who were interviewed practice Luskin's advice, even though it is unlikely that they are aware of his work. Social competency, empathy, and forgiveness can all greatly contribute to an individual's resilience.

Problem Solving and Planning

The ability to solve problems and effectively plan the future is another strong personal protective factor (Hassinger and Plourde 2005; Masten and Coatsworth 1998; Reis, Colbert, and Hébert 2005). Good problem-solving skills help a person think in an abstract manner and come up with alternative solutions to both cognitive and social problems. They then become comfortable asking others for help and advice. Benard (2004) describes problem solving as a "figuring-things-out-quality" linked to critical thinking.

Wolin and Wolin (1993) use the term *insight* to describe the same complex problem-solving process. They also found a strong link between insight and resilience. They theorize that during this process, children with high levels of resilience who are experiencing adversity, such as coping with a mother who inflicts physical abuse or a father with a mental disorder, often pose difficult questions to themselves based on their own observations. For instance, they may ask questions such as "where does my mother's anger come from?"

Because of their curious and inquisitive nature, they begin to observe more closely their abusive mother or ill father. They watch their interactions with other people and look for patterns and test their hypotheses. Wolin and Wolin (1993) call this *sensing.* Their sensing or "nose for trouble" leads to *knowing* or naming the situation for what it is (83). As these children are insightful, their knowing, as painful as it may be, helps them to achieve *understanding.*

Understanding the situation enables them to develop strategies and tools to survive in their often confusing and contradictory worlds. "Striving always to understand, resilient survivors process their experiences, look for meaning hidden beneath the surface of events, and confront themselves honestly" (Wolin and Wolin 1993, 81). One question they might ask is "what is this experience here to teach me?" This process allows individuals to strengthen their critical thinking skills because they are posing their own questions, an endeavor that according to Eisner (2002) is "the most intellectually demanding task" (579). Looking for meaning beneath the surface is an important step toward the development of a critical consciousness, a big step in problem solving.

Brooklyn, a twenty-one-year-old motivated, hard-working, and compassionate student illustrates problem solving and planning in action. She grew up in a devoutly religious home and in a strict church environment. Her father and mother were deeply dedicated and committed to the church and made it the foundation of their family's life and existence. Their world revolved around the teachings of their religion and how it applied to nearly every situation in their lives. As a child, Brooklyn was faced with the virtues and the restrictions of this world.

But over time her "inner voice" helped her understand how controlling this religious environment had become in her life. She states, "I saw how they [the members of the church] had damaged so many people and how they damaged me and [I] decided to change this and make it right." Brooklyn viewed the church as a serious problem in her life, an obstacle that she needed to confront. She began to distance herself from the influence, limit her contact, and develop plans to strike out in a new direction. After seventeen years of feeling judged and unaccepted, she took a huge personal risk. She decided to leave the church, even though she understood the deep personal pain her devout parents would feel as a result of her actions.

El Paso Community College played an important role in helping Brooklyn reorganize her life. There she planned an academic course of action, experienced new ideas, sought out different role models, and worked toward new goals. She set out on her own and began planning a career and a fuller, less restrictive life. Becoming more independent allowed her to seek greater challenges and broadened her horizons. New worlds opened up to her as she pursued her studies, especially in her psychology classes.

She was more drawn to the scientific view of the world and was impressed by her teachers. Dr. Carlos Amaya made Brooklyn's biology class particularly interesting. One psychology professor, Keith Pannell, arranged the course material of statistics, a subject that frightened her, into a manageable, meaningful process. He was able to explain complex formulas and guide students through a series of steps that led them to the correct answers. This helped Brooklyn develop a more organized, inquiring, scientific mind.

Brooklyn saw new role models at EPCC. She observed Hispanic professionals, especially women, who were confident, secure, intelligent, and dynamic. She visualized herself as one of these women and began to emulate their behaviors. Brooklyn decided to major in psychology and dreamed of becoming a college professor or a clinician. She developed a plan, consulted regularly with her teachers, and sought out a psychology professor as her mentor.

Brooklyn's life has greatly improved since she first enrolled in El Paso Community College. She completed her coursework and transferred to the University of Texas in El Paso. There she pursued advanced studies and earned a bachelor's degree in Psychology, graduating with honors. She also kept in touch with her EPCC teachers and regularly sought out their advice. These actions allowed her to develop a new, confident attitude, plan a career path, and become a new person.

She mended the relationship with her parents. They became supportive and enthusiastic about her new life and the goals she pursued. They proudly attended her graduation and honors ceremony, cheering her on. Brooklyn is currently a graduate student at the University of San Diego, pursuing a master's degree in Counseling, specializing in Clinical Mental Health. In 2016 she spent the summer studying abroad and traveling to exotic, romantic places throughout Europe. Brooklyn solved some serious personal problems and successfully laid out a plan for her life, exhibiting many of the characteristics of a resilient person.

Autonomy

Resilient individuals often exhibit autonomy, having a strong sense of self, identity, and power (Benard 2004). Autonomous individuals act independently and feel a sense of control over themselves and their environments. Autonomy is related to self-efficacy (Bandura 1997; Martin 2002). People with high levels of self-efficacy believe in their abilities and expect to achieve their goals. When self-efficacy is low, a person may choose not to pursue a goal, such as applying for a job or asking an attractive young lady out on a date.

Those who have low self-efficacy tend to view circumstances as more difficult than they really are and tend to dwell on their inadequacies (Bandura 1997). They often feel like "they don't measure up." But if self-efficacy is high, they pursue more challenging goals, such as choosing a competitive college major or working toward a promotion. Resilient individuals can develop higher self-efficacy and become confident in their ability to achieve their goals. It can provide an energy that helps them pursue new strategies and the resources necessary to be successful. This makes them feel that they have greater control over outcomes.

High self-efficacy can lead to self-awareness, which is characterized by an internal sense of control and an ability to recognize how emotions, thoughts, and actions affect us and those around us. Being self-aware and self-reflective, along with the ability to act on this awareness and reflection, is crucial in developing resilience (Morales 2000). For instance, individuals with a heightened sense of awareness can control their impulses and think beyond the moment. They may ask themselves, "What will my boss think if I am late to today's meeting?" or "How will studying for this test help with my career?" Individuals become keenly aware of the feelings, thoughts, and behaviors they project on to others. They understand that the way other people perceive them will impact their future.

Living resiliently also involves being aware of the weaknesses within that can hold people back. Social worker Nan Henderson describes an inner weakness as an Achilles's heel or "anything with the power to undo your life" (2012, 65). Weaknesses vary from individual to individual and can include many character traits, such as being too trusting or too guarded. They can also include addictive behaviors, such as overconsumption of alcohol, overspending, or overeating.

Some weaknesses can be entirely self-imposed or even imagined. Many El Paso Community College students are embarrassed by their language skills, fearing that they have a heavy accent when speaking English. They often speak English quite well, but have convinced themselves that they have a permanent disadvantage because of a perceived weakness. They tend to dismiss their own abilities and tell themselves that "their English is not good enough." There have been many times when students panic and confess that they cannot do a class presentation because they are not native English speakers and have had bad experiences in the past. This is what psychologists call a confirmational bias, which means that people often focus on experiences that reinforce their biases and beliefs.

If a teacher recognizes this Achilles's heel, he or she can reassure the students that their language skills are fine. He or she can create an atmosphere of excitement, show an interest in the topics the students will present, and move the focus away from the language and on to the content and presentation. It is also useful to remind the students that knowing two languages is a strength and that they are fortunate to be able to speak two languages in a world in which most people only speak one, a distinct advantage of living in a thriving border region. Resilient students understand their weaknesses but begin to look at them differently. Sometimes a perceived weakness needs considerable attention. It can also be turned into an asset and can help them move one step closer to autonomy.

As Brooklyn went through the process of solving personal problems and planning a career, she also developed autonomy. Several students struggled with strained relationships with their parents or family members who did not support their decisions or even approve of them attending college. Others felt pressure to work and generate income for the family rather than spend time in classes and accumulate expenses associated with earning a degree. This can be a normal part of an adolescent development, but in some cases it clashed with cultural values or attitudes such as *machismo* that interfered with women going to college or pursuing a career. Many students eventually developed a sense of autonomy, a way to exercise control and reduce some of the conflicts with others in their lives.

Autonomy can also be used to protect people from individuals who harm them physically, emotionally, or psychologically. Over time, they learn the importance of detaching or removing themselves from the source of their pain and suffering. Benard (2004) describes a strategy known as adaptive distancing, "realizing that one is not the cause of and cannot control the dysfunction of others" (25). Understanding that one did not cause the neglect or abuse inflicted on one or create the psychological illnesses of their loved ones can be a great challenge and may take a lifetime to achieve.

Autonomy can be cultivated slowly and gradually, step by step, while solving problems, planning, and experiencing new approaches to life. Amanda, an eighteen-year-old Hispanic female, developed a close mentoring relationship with her Education 1300 professor and used the course as a way to enhance her personal autonomy, a vital step in becoming resilient. The first-year experience class helped her work through basic academic goals, such as identifying potential careers, assessing her strengths and weaknesses, and making decisions on her own. The decisions were sometimes contrary to the wishes of her family. Her parents were supportive and nurturing, but had never been to college and did not understand some of the choices she needed to make or some of the complexities of different careers and programs of study.

Amanda felt an inordinate amount of pressure because she is the oldest of four children. Her path through college would lead the way for her younger siblings and could become a model for success. Amanda focused on small, specific tasks that would help with her studies. She learned to pay close attention to the course syllabus so that she understood exactly what was expected and how she could plan for assignments.

She gained control of her studies by applying many concepts she had learned in her Education 1300 class. For example, there never seemed to be enough time for everything in her life. At home there was always a sense of chaos and urgency. Amanda discovered that one could gain autonomy through time management and began to apply the basic principles to her life at home, personal relations, work, and studies.

Her parents wanted her to follow a rather traditional course of study: to be an elementary school teacher. But Amanda also had other interests and hoped to pursue them at the university. She supplemented her studies with courses in creative writing, psychology, and counseling.

Amanda wanted to attend New Mexico State University, forty miles away, rather than the University of Texas at El Paso, so that she could select from a greater variety of fields of study.

Her parents saw this as a frivolous expense, time-consuming, and counterproductive. But Amanda was able to use her time management skills, new knowledge of debt, investment, and money, and study skills, knowledge she had acquired in her first-year experience class, to make it work. She found a part-time job, purchased a reliable vehicle, borrowed a small amount of money, and set off for New Mexico, the Land of Enchantment. Amanda had developed autonomy. She could make decisions, present a persuasive argument to her family, and follow through on her plans. Amanda eventually graduated, became a certified public school teacher, and is now pursuing graduate studies.

A Sense of Purpose

Ultimately, resilient people find their place in the world and develop a larger sense of purpose. Carl Jung, a Swiss psychiatrist and psychotherapist who founded analytical psychology, claims that the ultimate goal is to become whole, or who we are meant to be. Jung called this process *individuation* and describes it as a transformation of the psyche that results from integrating and bringing the personal and collective unconscious into consciousness. The process of individuation leads toward wholeness or undividedness of personality and the self (Mattoon 2005).

Jung argues that many physical and mental distresses come from repressing the true essence of an individual. This is particularly common in early adulthood, when so many students struggle with college and at the same time try establishing their own identity and leading a new life. Parents and loved ones often have difficulty letting go. They keep trying to shape a child's life long after they have proven that they can make their own decisions and act responsibly. They may attempt to control their destiny by imposing their own ideas of who they should be rather than fostering spaces where the child can access his or her own inner voice. Being resilient means recognizing that each person is their own being with their own calling and having the courage to express this uniqueness.

Benard defines sense of purpose as "the deep belief that one's life has meaning and that one has a place in the universe" (2004, 28). It is the answer to the question "Why was I born?" She describes sense of purpose as an overarching concept, one that encompasses goal direction, educational aspirations, creativity, optimism, and meaning. Like Brooklyn and Amanda, individuals with a strong sense of purpose often have specific goals and detailed plans, along with the persistence to succeed. This can ultimately lead to finding a calling, a place in the world where they belong and can achieve well-being and happiness.

Human beings are hard-wired to be resilient, as witnessed in the intuitive and creative problem-solving nature of children (Henderson 2012). It is amazing to watch a five-year-old child use Lego pieces to improvise and create intergalactic worlds with secrets, languages, and forms of power that are unknown to common earthlings. Most people, if they think deeply, can probably recall similar activities from their own childhood, even if the toys were sticks and stones rather than fancy electronic store-bought gadgets.

Something changes over time and, as people mature, much of this wonder and creativity is lost. Some believe that adults today desperately need to tap into the abilities that were once second nature but have diminished over the years. In many professional jobs that once encouraged innovation and creativity, people are subjected to standardization, routine, and monotony. Regaining creativity can lead to autonomy and a larger sense of purpose.

Combining autonomy and empathy can lead to altruism, the act of helping others without expecting anything in return, and heighten the sense of purpose. A person with empathy for someone else is much more likely to offer help in some way (Snyder and Lopez 2007, 268). People who are altruistic may assist an individual person in a moment of need or they might help an entire community or fight for a larger cause. Empathy and altruism, the acts of understanding and making a difference in the lives of others, can also lead to advocacy, especially when influenced by the ideology of social justice.

Two students who exude altruism and have developed a true sense of purpose are Guadalupe and Valentina. They were both born and raised in Ciudad Juárez and both suffered from difficult childhoods. They were raised by parents who abused alcohol and they endured many years of neglect and physical and emotional abuse. Valentina and Guadalupe are now in their thirties and have teenage children. Guadalupe can be characterized as being reflective and one who engages in deep thinking, while Valentina is outgoing with a great sense of humor.

They met when they enrolled for ESL classes at El Paso Community College. Because of their similar struggles and the "same hunger and passion to help those in need," they bonded instantly and now thrive off of each other's energy and commitment. They are *como uña y mugre*. Their kinship is as tight as the nail and the dirt that lives underneath it. Through their early studies at EPCC, they sharpened their sense of purpose and developed altruistic values. As they read and researched topics, such as immigration rights, human trafficking, and abuses of children, they became aware of many pressing social problems in their own community:

> Guadalupe: Something happened to me and my way of thinking. I think it made me more critical and skeptical, *me amalicie*. It made me aware of so many horrible things that go on while we are living our ordinary lives—raising our children, working, going to school. We are surrounded by this. I also realized that we have people who are enslaved living in this country. They are being threatened and harmed in order to keep them enslaved. Who knows? We may even have people that live in our city that are enslaved. Sometimes when I see a man mistreating a woman I think, "Maybe she is enslaved?"

Valentina and Guadalupe's learning developed in them a sense of altruism, bolstered their resilience, and led them on new career pathways. They decided to become social workers after they learned that "social workers fight for people's rights, human rights." Even though they both have families to raise, full-time jobs, and continue to take classes, they find the time to help new immigrants in ministry work at their church. They have become interested in the rights of children, especially those who "live in alcoholic homes and don't have any advocates or people looking out for them."

Valentina and Guadalupe's motivation to excel in their courses at EPCC was underpinned by their newfound altruism, an awareness that the knowledge and resources they acquire can help transform the lives of the families throughout their community. This gave them a clear sense of purpose and meaning. Valentina and Guadalupe were also able to forgive their parents for their abusive alcoholic past and neglect. They never condoned or dismissed the pain and suffering they had endured during their most critical developmental years, childhood and adolescence. But their forgiveness was an act of rejuvenation and led to a new and fresh relationship.

After achieving a state of forgiveness, they were able to interact with their parents differently. They were also able to move forward, as resilient people do, and go above and beyond the call of duty to provide and care for their parents and families. Valentina and Guadalupe graduated in May 2015 after six challenging years at El Paso Community College. During their graduation celebration, they read letters of gratitude they had written to their parents and loved ones. The tears of joy and love and laughter projected in their voices were a testament to how much healing these students and their families had

achieved. Basic social competency, the development of empathy and relationships, altruism, and forgiveness can help define a sense of purpose.

Mindfulness, Elements, and the Pursuit of Happiness

Community college students often respond well to popular literature that
shows how these fundamental behaviors and habits can truly change people's
lives. With rather simple exercises, they can see beyond the psychological
theories to find something more concrete and more directly applicable to
their own lives. One exercise is mindfulness. Jon Kabat-Zinn (2012) pio-
neered medical studies of meditation in the 1980s, many based on Buddhist
beliefs and practices. This provided the basis for later studies of mindfulness.
Mindfulness is based on forms of meditation and concentration, focusing and
savoring attention on experiences in the present moment. Mindfulness has
been associated with long-term well-being and health and has been shown to
be useful in reducing depression, stress, and anxiety.

While building autonomy, an individual can develop his or her sense of
mindfulness. Through mindfulness, students can focus on and discover new
aspects of themselves. They can enter a new state of awareness and greatly
expand their sense of purpose in the world. Eckhart Tolle's *A New Earth:
Awakening to Your Life's Purpose* challenges readers to use mindfulness to
ask themselves one of the most fundamental questions: Who am I? He explains that "knowing yourself goes far deeper than the adoption of a set of
ideas or beliefs" (2005, 186). Tolle points out that most people know themselves only in terms of their past and future and spend much of their time
dwelling on what has happened and what might happen. They should instead
focus on "being," an awareness of the present moment, rather than getting
lost in the past and future of their minds. Tolle argues that once a person is
mindful they become more aware of their strengths, weaknesses, and abilities.

Living a resilient life means becoming more mindful and alert when
facing challenging situations. Mindfulness strengthens consciousness, which
then enlightens the individual and leads to a state of alertness or awareness, a
state of "being." Mindfulness, or a state of being, has been described as a
presence in the moment, being aware of the surroundings and stimuli and
consciousness of one's place in the world. Most people are subject to distractions, thoughts that clutter their minds and cause them to miss out on the
simplest and most fundamental elements of their lives. They lack focus or
concentration. Tolle states that they should instead be noticing small, common things in greater numbers and variety. This state of awareness can allow
people to experience the rich qualities of everyday life and find more of those
qualities everywhere.

Simple exercises can teach students to focus on these everyday details and help them become more "mindful" of their own worlds. For example, they might notice the sweetness of every sip from a steaming hot cup of black tea each morning. A leisurely walk might lead to inspiration, as the shifting formations created by the sunlight gently sweep through the clouds and cast shadows on the ground. The light scent of sprawling laurels that adorn a neighbor's yard and the colorful, layered shades of pink that live in these flowers can draw one in further. Mindfulness can keep stray thoughts about the past or future at bay, opening the mind to new experiences.

Mindfulness reveals how much there is to appreciate in the world, and this appreciation is often followed by a sense of gratitude. Tolle relates that "acknowledging the good that is already in your life is the foundation for all abundance" (2005, 190). Gratitude helps one to stay in the present moment. Therefore mindfulness and gratitude work in synchrony to enhance self-awareness. The opposite is also true. If the human mind lives constantly in the past and future and the focus is on trivial matters, its existence becomes trivial. Tolle warns that "if the small things have the power to disturb you, then who you think you are is exactly that: small" (2005, 187).

Being mindful and focusing on the present can help a person discover their elements, the places where they can exercise their natural ability or interest, something that they can build over time and nurture as an aptitude, skill, or career. Discovering one's elements can also greatly enhance autonomy and cultivate a sense of purpose. In *Finding your Element*, Ken Robinson, internationally recognized leader in the development of creativity, argues that the modern world is one of distractions in which the constant pull of the external world (smartphones, data, laptops, the Internet, and television) draws us away from the internal world and encourages "rapid response rather than deep engagement and critical reflection" (2013, 7).

Constant inundations of new information limit the ability to analyze or critically appraise that information. He suggests that inundation can be controlled and slowed down. In doing so, a person can be alone with themselves and concentrate on entering the "flow of their own being." Robinson argues that in order to regain basic skills, such as critical thinking and reflection, skills that are vital to autonomy and problem solving, an individual needs to enter this state in which his or her talents meet his or her passions, where he or she can tame wild emotions, calm him- or herself down, and eliminate noises that clutter thinking.

Something as simple as savoring, meditation, prayer, gratitude, and other "mindfulness" practices or activities, such as gardening, drawing, and mind mapping, can make a big difference. Robinson believes that only through this process can someone truly find his or her place, a place in which he or she is doing something for which he or she "[has] a natural feel," in which "natural aptitude meets personal passion" (2013, xi). This is his or her element, in which thoughts and skills can thrive, a place that is comfortable, inviting, and stimulating. Students learn that the element is a place where potential, creativity, and results are maximized.

Once someone enters his or her element and is enjoying the process, he or she still has to do the work. World-renowned Harvard psychologist Howard Gardner (1983) developed his theory of multiple intelligences as a result of studying the lives of extraordinary people with creative minds, people who were clearly in their element. Gardner found that even though they were born with great aptitude, they still had to work very hard at turning those aptitudes into skills and products. It took well-known geniuses such as Mozart, Picasso, and Einstein about ten years to truly become expert composers, artists, and scientists. Students are intrigued by Gardner's ideas and can often apply the theories to their own learning styles and academic pursuits.

Malcolm Gladwell popularized this idea in his best seller *Outliers*, in which he explains that geniuses are made rather than born. He cites many studies to show that even though genes do play an important role in innate ability, natural talent is not enough to become a grand master. Gladwell argues that becoming an expert requires the ability to stay focused for a long period of time and to practice skills with the purpose of getting better. He introduces the idea of ten thousand hours as a "magic number of greatness," a period of time in which skills are truly mastered and the individual's creativity can excel (2008, 41).

Gary McPherson found that vision, the ability to see oneself in the future with mastery and accomplishment, was often the difference between semi-successful musicians and truly exemplary performers (Coyle 2009). He notes that a simple question like "How long do you think you will play?" is a good predictor of the level of success a student will achieve. Those with visions of themselves as lifelong musicians did exactly that—over time they became "great." Those who hesitated in answering or saw themselves studying for a few years and then moving on to other interests did exactly that. The visionaries who invested ten thousand hours savored the process. Even though it takes time, persistence, and hard work to develop talents, those who have become experts often describe how this enjoyable process continues to be vital to their success.

Students are encouraged to be more mindful, enter a state of flow, and seek out their elements (Csikszentmihalyi 1996). But the experience does not have to be entirely enjoyable. In fact, some studies have actually established a link between adversity and creativity. Simonton (2000) concludes that exceptional creativity does not always emerge from nurturing environments. It appears to require exposure to occasional hardship to strengthen the individual's capacity to overcome difficult situations. Simonton adds that "some of the most adverse childhoods can give birth to the most creative adulthoods"; in other words, no pain, no gain (2000, 153).

David Brooks supports Simonton's findings. In *The Social Animal*, he writes about a connection between "ultra-driven people" and a "deep sense of existential danger." Brooks says that "historians have long noticed that an astonishing percentage of the greatest writers, musicians, artists, and leaders had a parent die or abandon them while they were between the ages of nine and fifteen . . . the loss that occurred early in their life provided a sense of urgency, anxiety, and impetus that propelled them to achieve" (2011, 133). People as diverse as George Washington, Thomas Jefferson, Alexander Hamilton, Abraham Lincoln, Adolph Hitler, Gandhi, and Stalin experienced this adversity and in some ways benefited from it. Some community college students who have faced personal tragedies or losses are comforted by the fact that such setbacks do not necessarily mean that their academic careers are over. Through perseverance they can become more resilient and eventually get back on track.

Building social competence, autonomy, developing problem-solving skills, and finding your element, along with a strong sense of purpose, can ultimately lead to a state of fulfillment and psychological wellness or happiness. Many students are fascinated by the recent wave of happiness studies, studies that illustrate how happiness develops and how it can be cultivated and nurtured during a lifetime.

Positive psychologist Sonja Lyubomirsky (2007) found that happiness and well-being are within most people's reach and that they are closely connected to meaning. She notes that 50 percent of happiness is heritable or attributed to genetic factors. Despite what most people think, life circumstances such as being rich, being beautiful, getting married, buying a larger house, driving a state-of-the-art sports car, or even indulging in extensive plastic surgeries account for a very small portion of happiness, only about 10 percent.

A whopping 40 percent of happiness is determined by intentional daily activities that are usually within a person's control (Lyubomirsky 2007). In other words, the key to happiness or finding meaning is not necessarily limited by genetic makeup (that cannot be controlled) or by major changes in life circumstances (that are usually impractical or even impossible to achieve). Happiness is usually determined by how lives are lived, day after day, year after year.

Unfortunately, most people focus on life circumstances and are disappointed with the results. Part of the reason is due to a phenomenon known as hedonic adaptation, our ability to adapt quickly to changes in life circumstances. Many people experience instant gratification, a burst of pleasure when something changes, and then they adapt, which makes the change seem transient and fleeting. As someone hedonically adapts, they set a new, higher baseline and seek more pleasure. It simply feels like they never have enough, they never achieve enough, and they never reach the level to which they aspire.

Almost immediately, people set new, higher expectations and begin pursuing them. There is a sort of buyer's remorse; the life circumstance almost feels like a disappointment. Dr. Lyubomirsky and others have found that overall physical, psychological, and spiritual well-being is determined by engaging in behaviors and activities that slow down the adaptation process and allow one to develop meaning. Activities such as expressing gratitude, practicing acts of kindness, and fostering resilience and optimism can produce meaning even under the direst circumstances.

Extrinsic goals (earning more money or accumulating more products) should be seen as part of a process, a stepping stone toward achieving intrinsic goals (developing autonomy, a strong sense of purpose, pursuing life goals, dreams, and aspirations). Intrinsic goals require persistence and perseverance and, in the long run, are far more rewarding because they allow one "to grow as a person, to develop emotional maturity, and to contribute to a community" (Lyubomirsky 2007, 208).

These can be modest goals, such as learning to play a musical instrument, drawing, or studying a new language, or they can be big purposeful goals, such as mastering a craft or developing a vision. In the first-year experience courses, understanding these basics can help students pursue more focused, realistic goals. They learn that as they plan their careers and their lives, they should concentrate more on meaning, the intrinsic goal that can ultimately secure their happiness and well-being.

Personal memoirs and fictionalized accounts can also bring many of these ideas to life in the classroom. In Mitch Albom's (1997) classic memoir *Tuesdays with Morrie*, he vividly portrays the way in which the student-teacher dynamic can bring all of this together. Morrie, an exuberant, exciting professor of sociology, became Mitch's mentor, guided him through his formative years, helped him launch a successful broadcast career, and at a subconscious level helped mold his values and influenced his decisions. Although the professor remained an inspiration and role model, they lost touch over the years and went their separate ways. Mitch savored his success, enjoyed his new professional life, and saw less and less of Morrie.

Later Mitch found out that Morrie had become ill with ALS, a debilitating neurological condition, and was in the last months of his life. Morrie had always encouraged his students to work hard and expected much of them. Mitch decided to embark on one final but extremely challenging project with Morrie, capturing and documenting his last days and celebrating his profound, uplifting, warm, and incandescent spirit. Mitch remained fascinated by his perseverance and spirit but was uncomfortable and anxious with where the journey was leading him. With Morrie's condition increasingly deteriorating, their conversations got progressively more intense.

After a while, Mitch summoned up the courage to ask, "How can anyone ever be prepared to die?" Morrie explained that even though everyone knows they are going to die some day, few people truly believe it. "If we did we would do things differently." Morrie suggests that everyone should start preparing early in their lives. He encouraged his puzzled student:

> Do what the Buddhists do. Every day, have a little bird on your shoulder that asks, "Is today the day? Am I ready? Am I doing all I need to do? Am I being the person I want to be?" (Albom 1997, 81)

Morrie then "turned his head to his shoulder as if the bird were there now." "Is today the day I die?" he asked. Morrie was trying to answer his questions but was also trying to, as always, push his student further. Healthy doses of anxiety generate the inertia that often propels us to act and behave in ways that are necessary to fulfill our visions.

Mitch's determination to honor Morrie by narrating his beloved professor's life had a purpose. Mitch's work held urgency to it; he was overwhelmed, not sure where this would take him, and was being mentored by a man whose time was running out. By being a part of Morrie's life, he envisioned a larger purpose. He was on a search for meaning, a search that lies at the core of every human heart. Educational goals and meaning need to develop over time. This can be accomplished by absorbing new experiences, attitudes, and behaviors early in the process when one goes to college and is exposed to myriad thoughts and beliefs.

Every student hopes to find a mentor like Morrie and every teacher hopes to be Morrie. Resilient students use persistence and creativity to find relevance, lead meaningful lives, and become whole. Mitch is a fine example of how someone develops resilience through personal protective factors. He gained autonomy, had a sense of purpose, developed a vision, followed a step-by-step plan, and found meaning in his life.

Chapter Two

Environmental Protective Factors and Teacher Qualities

Personal protective factors build better resilience in a nurturing environment. The immediate environments of family, school, and community, which shape a significant part of our lives, can serve as additional protective factors, allowing our internal strengths to grow (Benard 2004). Studies of "at-risk" populations have consistently found that family, school experiences, peer interaction, and community can be very reliable factors that influence and determine the well-being of individuals (Haggerty et al. 1994). They can protect young people from the effects of exposure to risk and help them "beat the odds" and "succeed despite a situation that usually implies failure" (Wayman 2002, 168).

These environments can greatly aid in the development of individuals if they are "rich in caring relationships, high expectations, and opportunities for meaningful participation and contribution" (Benard 2004, 107). Together strong personal and environmental protective factors serve as powerful buffers and can help prevent a person from undergoing a downward spiral, resulting in complete despair when coping with difficult or traumatic experiences.

FAMILY AS AN ENVIRONMENTAL PROTECTIVE FACTOR

Families can help individuals by providing them with support and high expectations (Garza et al. 2004). The research overwhelmingly demonstrates that "consistent supportive and responsive parenting is among the most robust predictor of children's well-being" (Luthar and Zelazo 2003, 520). Caring relationships with parents, members of the family, or other adults are

beneficial because they help to shape the individuals' development and provide a sense of trust and security. Establishing trust with a caring adult is a
building block that can later lead to very rewarding and positive relationships
with teachers, mentors, or peers who can influence their success (Lambie et
al. 2002).

Wolin and Wolin (1993) explain that we explore and develop self-concept in the same way that we learn to use a mirror. When we are born, we are
"small, naked, and ignorant," but we soon "piece together a picture of ourselves—first of our bodies, and then of our essential nature—by seeing our
reflection in the faces of the people who take care of us" (16). These mirrors
reflect a reality and can work in very positive or very negative ways. Children who "generally see love, approval, pleasure, and admiration in the mirror of their parents' faces construct a corresponding inner representation of
themselves that says, 'I am lovable. I am good.'"

However, in afflicted families, "the mirroring process goes awry, and
children are at risk of forming an inner representation of themselves that
says, 'I am ugly. I am unacceptable.'" Often these troubled families who are
"twisted and bent out of shape" are "like a distorted mirror that reflects
grotesque images" (Wolin and Wolin 1993, 17).

Fortunately, negative reflections do not always have negative consequences. As people become resilient, they can recognize that something is
not quite right in their reflection. Then they seek an alternate one in which
the image is more pleasing and appealing (Wolin and Wolin 1993).

For many the search for a more positive reflection can take place throughout their life as they interact with new people and experience new environments. They may become close with a relative or acquaintance or they may
simply observe from a distance and begin to develop a new, more positive
reflection.

EPCC student Luís explains how his father mirrored and modeled resilience for him throughout his childhood. He describes his father, Mr. Luna, as
"a man who stood six-feet-two inches tall and weighed 250 pounds," with a
physical appearance similar to "a mighty wrestler on the tube," who towered
over his small wife. But this giant became as weak as a "newborn fawn"
when diagnosed with Guillian-Barre syndrome, a rare disorder in which the
immune system attacks the nerves and can eventually paralyze the entire
body.

The exact cause was unknown but it left him quadriplegic for almost ten
years. Then he "miraculously, began to move and eventually walk again. He
wore braces on his legs and used a cane to help support his weight when he
walked." Luís remembers his father as being "a kind, giving, just man . . .
who was strict but joked around a lot. He would not hesitate to lend a hand,
give up the shirt on his back or the shoes on his feet" when he saw someone

in need. Luís remembers many instances of how his father helped other people:

> My dad would give to people whatever it was they needed: food, shelter, advice, money, physical help, or a simple joke. He would give and give and not expect anything in return. One time he gave away my mom's brand new, one-week-old corduroy couches to a struggling family. Good Lord did he sleep in the dog house for a long time, but as he put it, "It was well worth it." Many times he upset my mom and all his children because there were times when we would have to give up our toys. The phone often rang in the middle of the night. My dad would pray for people over the phone.

Luís admires and mirrors his father's sense of humor. Even in the most difficult times, people enjoyed the company of Mr. Luna because he always had a joke to tell. At one point in his illness, his legs had to be amputated just below the hip. Luís could not believe the strength and courage his father had summoned during the ordeal. He knew that if this had been him, he would have been devastated, but his father was still "cracking jokes about his situation, as if nothing had happened."

The day after the surgery, Luís and his mother anxiously entered the hospital room, unsure of what they would say or how they would respond. But before they could utter a word, his dad looked at his mother, smiled, and said, "*¡Mira Vieja!* We are now the same height!" Luís and his mother immediately "lost it." They "had tears of sorrow mixed with tears of joy." After enduring this incredible tragedy, Mr. Luna was more concerned about the well-being of his family than his own personal pain and suffering. Luís learned from his father how to "make lemonade when life hands you lemons." Mr. Luna shed whatever machismo or egotism he may have had left and was never afraid to express his true feelings through acts of kindness.

Luís married his life companion, Carla, and together they mirror much of his parents' relationship. They are currently attending EPCC, taking their classes together and supporting each other's academic and emotional needs. Luís is a school bus driver and is going to become a school counselor, while Carla is majoring in accounting. They are both in their late twenties and are very proud parents of their two-year-old daughter, Lily. Providing a better future for their daughter and making their loving father, Mr. Luna, proud is what motivates them to do high-quality work in their classes. His father "is the most influential" person in Luís's life. He has helped Luís develop his self-concept. Throughout his upbringing, the Luna family has been a mirror that has reflected love, strength, kindness, and joy for Luís.

What happens when individuals are not provided with the type of parenting they need? The reflections provided by our families or other people in our lives who function in unhealthy ways do not always have negative consequences. The Wolins (1993) explain that unhealthy messages can indeed lead to a lifelong journey of pain and pathologies, but they may also challenge us to break free from this spell and seek "alternate mirrors" that will offer a more "pleasing image" of ourselves. This was the case for David, who was abandoned by his father and was raised by his mother, who neglected him. He sought alternate mirrors and began the process of creating a new reflection, a composite of individuals who helped him through his early life.

David was often left on his own, having to perform the most basic tasks by himself. His mother paid little attention to his needs. For example, she seldom prepared regular meals or made sure that he was being properly fed. At an early age, David had to fend for himself. Over time, he became more resourceful, performing basic tasks like ensuring that he had food to eat. In fact, by the age of fourteen he had learned how to take care of himself quite well; for instance, he could prepare his own meals. He "ended up learning how to cook over 20 different types of dishes that ranged from mac and cheese to meatball soup and chicken Alfredo."

David was an introverted, inquisitive, and respectful boy, but had trouble socializing at school. He never quite fit in, and during his middle school years, he was bullied, threatened, and one time even robbed by other students. He also felt that he was being shamed by some of his teachers. Fortunately, David had other family members who presented a better reflection for him and influenced his development and growth. While his mother was preoccupied or absent, his grandparents stepped in to provide support and nurture him. David began to see how his mother's "mirror" was causing so many of his problems and how his grandparents became alternates who had the time, the temperament, and the wisdom to guide him.

Over the years, David realized that when he had the opportunity, he needed to move on. He said, "I had so many issues with my mom that I ended up breaking that chain and cutting all ties with her. After I graduated from high school I decided to move in with my grandparents." They provided a much better environment for David so that he could continue with his life and enroll at EPCC. Once there he began to encounter others who provided a better reflection and had a positive influence on his development.

He joined Mr. Richard Yañez's writing course through the Puente Project, a program at EPCC that helps at-risk Mexican American students' transition to college. During his first semester, David struggled to keep up and was barely getting passing grades on his assignments. Mr. Yañez kept a close eye on him and supported him in his studies. He foresaw David's potential and encouraged him, especially after observing how much effort David was putting into the final exam. Mr. Yañez told David he was coming along and said, "I know you're going to pass next semester easily now, because you're a person that just continues to evolve."

David had met an alternate mirror. Mr. Yañez spent countless hours talking to him and working through his problems. David developed a deep admiration for him and began to see him as a "mentor" and "father figure"; an extension of family. He said that the experience "energized" him, "piqued his interest," and provided him with a sense of hope. He saw other positive qualities in people whom he met through Puente, such as Chicano literary figures and prominent guest speakers who created a new image of what a "real man" looks like. He also began to mirror their intellectual curiosity, something he had lacked in his high school years.

He was particularly captivated by feminist author bell hooks and her seminal work *Feminism Is for Everybody* (2014):

> The more I read about bell hooks the more I ended up getting thoughts and ideas, which honestly got me frustrated, but in a good way, because it made me want to learn more. It ended up sparking my critical thinking and opened up my eyes to what feminism is and that guys like me can make a big impact in changing the world.

Families can also provide great motivation and high expectations. Angel's early schooling was problematic, with little family support or encouragement. His mother, Ms. Gomez, was a very hard worker who held two jobs in order to raise him and his sister. As an uneducated, unskilled immigrant, she had few opportunities, but always took whatever work was available. She endured long hours at demanding jobs for little pay in order to make ends meet, but always made sure that the family was well provided for.

His mother simply kept plodding along, working at a manufacturing plant and at a plastic injection molding factory, earning enough for the family's basic needs. Unfortunately, there were many limitations on the role she played in Angel's education. Ms. Gomez knew little about the school system and seldom had the time to engage in academic or supporting activities. Like many poor single parents, she was unable to provide her children with extracurricular activities or extensive social contact. Angel drifted in school, lost focus, and eventually dropped out. He made several attempts to return to his studies with mixed results.

But Angel's life took a strange turn when, in his mid-twenties, he became a father and began to think about the impact of these failures on his son. Supporting a wife and child with a low-paying service job was a daunting task, and he knew that the only way he could provide for his family in the long run was by completing his education and thereby having better employment opportunities. In the midst of this struggle, Angel's mother viewed his life as reaching a point of crisis and decided to intervene to help him survive and overcome the mistakes that he had made in the past.

She provided a more supportive environment, one that helped with his expenses and encouraged him to pursue a college degree. She instilled a basic hard work ethic and mirrored positive traits that helped him build

resilience and succeed. She concentrated on his day-to-day needs and strongly encouraged Angel to work more diligently, pay attention to his teachers,
and concentrate on his classes.

Angel enrolled at El Paso Community College. Ms. Gomez supported
him financially and provided motivation. She purchased his textbooks, allowed him to borrow her car, and encouraged him to stay focused. She spoke
more of school as an opportunity, not an obligation or chore, and enthusiastically supported his studies. Despite hardships and limited resources, Angel
did not experience a childhood of extreme deprivation or great emotional
stress. He had access to the basics needed to succeed, but his own decisions
held him back. Later in life, his family was able to create a more nurturing
and motivating environment, providing him with a strong protective factor
and helping him pursue his dreams.

Several families in this study have provided similar support. Although
they had limited formal education, they understood that schooling is essential
to succeed and acquire stability. They lovingly supported their children and
provided what little they could to promote their success.

SCHOOL AS AN ENVIRONMENTAL PROTECTIVE FACTOR

When parents and family members are not available, other adults, such as
teachers, counselors, and members of the school community, may provide
the affection, support, and assistance that help to promote resilience (Gonzalez and Padilla 1997; Lambie et al. 2002). A combination of caring teachers
and supportive peers in school can provide students with a strong sense of
belonging, a safe environment that becomes an important component of their
academic success. Students who feel they are part of a school community are
less likely to become disengaged or to lack purpose. When interacting with
their peers and teachers, they experience a sense of belonging and accep-
tance.

Without it, students can feel alone and adrift, lose focus, and drop out of
school. Resilient students often describe how an individual teacher or fellow
student broke the ice, welcomed them into the college community, and made
them feel at home in an unfamiliar campus, a large classroom, or a new
program of study.

Biology professor Danny Flores (pseudonym) is well known at El Paso
Community College for his caring personality and great sense of humor,
which he uses to put students at ease and welcome them to his classes. He
fully understands that science and math can be among the most frightening
subjects for college students, and he uses his sense of humor to alleviate their
anxiety and to make them feel at home. He shared the following:

On the very first day of class we go over the syllabus and all the rules, and I'll say, "Guys, you know what? I don't think of me as professor, you student, you stay over there" (uses hands to show distance). I say, "No, no, no, no, no." I tell them sincerely and honestly, from my heart, "I think of us as family." We are a family that gets together every Monday, Wednesday, Friday for an hour and we talk biology. "And so I'm like the crazy uncle, okay? We'll laugh at the good jokes, but then we'll cry at the bad ones."

Mr. Flores, an experienced community college professor, treats his students like family because he understands what the research has shown: caring teachers are the most significant factor for students' academic achievement (Ferguson 1991; Sanders and Rivers 1996; Strauss and Sawyer 1986). They are the most influential element in the greater school community. By letting his guard down and being genuinely interested, Mr. Flores is able to motivate them. The research confirms that students "not only learn from a teacher but also for a teacher" if the emotional connection is there (Delpit 2006, 227).

Students want their teachers to know that they are working just as hard, have the same interests in the course, and want to perform well, not just for themselves but so that teachers like Mr. Flores receive the same reinforcement and encouragement to continue their great work. A recent Gallup-Purdue Index report of thirty thousand graduates of American colleges found that students who connected with a professor who "stimulated them, cared about them, and encouraged their hopes and dreams" doubled the chances of being engaged in their work and were three times as likely to thrive (Carlson 2014, 1).

Many of the EPCC students interviewed agreed with the findings of the Gallup-Purdue Index report about "great teaching." A common response was that great professors are extremely knowledgeable, demonstrate a love, enthusiasm, and respect for their discipline, and connect with students in ways that make them want to learn. Alejandra thought that the best teachers are "those who never forgot they were once a student" because they hold high standards and yet are "understanding and compassionate." They know how to present material in an organized, manageable form but are very thorough in their expertise. Brooklyn loved professors who told students their own stories of adversity, struggle, and resilience in order to inspire them.

Teachers create a comfortable environment in which their students can thrive. For Jorge, a great teacher is someone "who gives you the tools to create your own ideas." Guadalupe expressed the following when describing her and Valentina's experiences with Dr. Myshie Pagel and Ms. Rose Galindo, their ESL writing and reading professors:

Even though they have different personalities they have one thing in common. They do not see *enseñanza* [pedagogy] as a job. They see it as their life. They have shown us this over and over. They were always willing to help us. They

would worry about our progress. They always wanted to know how we were
doing. We would run into them in the hall and they would ask, "How are you
doing in your other classes?"

Valentina added that both of their professors offered to help her and Guadalupe with work from their other classes, even if this was not the area they
taught.

When they would say, "Bring me your essays and we will sit down and work
on them" that really made me admire and respect them. I know that they do not
have to do that. That is not part of their job. They don't get paid extra, but they
do this out of love for their students and for their profession. They leave the
classroom and they leave the building and they continue being *maestras*
[teachers].

The opposite is also true. Students commented that poor teachers are
those "who saw teaching as nothing but a paycheck," did not care if students
passed or failed, never bothered to learn their names, and "treated them like
they were just a number." Some reported teachers who knew little of the
subject matter, discouraged questions and discussions, and were often confused about some of the basic concepts taught in the class. As a result,
students felt disengaged in such an unwelcoming space.

Disengagement, or worse, avoidance, puts students at risk of performing
poorly, learning less, failing courses, and ultimately dropping out of college.
Unfortunately, the Gallup-Purdue report revealed that American colleges
overall fell short on human connectedness, a measurement that these EPCC
students found particularly important. "While 63 percent of respondents said
they had encountered professors who got them fired up about a subject," only
"27 percent had had professors who cared about them, and 22 percent had
found mentors who encouraged them" (Carlson 2014, 1).

Valenzuela (1999) believes that authentic care, which views relationships
between students and teachers as the basis for learning, is important when
teaching Mexican Americans because it parallels the Mexican understanding
of *educación*, or education. Educación is "a model of schooling premised on
respectful, caring relationships" and is much broader than the American concept of education (61). Valenzuela (1999) explains that educacíon is much
bigger than the school campus or setting; "it also refers to the family's role of
inculcating in the children a sense of moral, social, and personal responsibility," which "serves as the foundation for all other learning" (23).

Benard (2004) agrees and writes that at the "core of caring relationships
are clear and positive expectations that not only structure and guide behavior
but also challenge students beyond what they believe" (73). Even when the
education system as a whole does not expect much from its students, relationships with individual teachers who convey high expectations serve as a

powerful predictor of successful outcomes. Nieto (2004) further states that "care means loving students in the most profound ways: through high expectations, great support, and rigorous demands" (270). It is important that these rigorous demands are carried out in a warm and respectful manner in a trusting classroom setting in which community has been established.

These expectations must also be accompanied by opportunities for students to interact and contribute in meaningful ways. Caring teachers often engage students in experiential or hands-on learning in order to strengthen their autonomy, problem-solving skills, social competence, and sense of purpose. Benard (2004) notes that experiential learning that emphasizes the importance of relationships, is collaborative in nature, and is paired with high expectations is particularly effective. This is not only meaningful for students, but also promotes their educational resilience. In this way, teachers, such as Danny Flores and Richard Yañez, make the educational setting and process of schooling an environmental protective factor, one that has greatly added to the development of resilient students at EPCC.

COMMUNITY AS AN ENVIRONMENTAL PROTECTIVE FACTOR

Communities can serve as powerful environmental factors. It is very common for individuals to develop a connection to, become more engaged in, and eventually want to give something back to their communities. They see their communities as a nurturing environment that helped protect and develop them over the years. In time, they want to offer others the same assistance and support that they benefited from. Resilient individuals derive a strong sense of meaning from this process of "giving back," a sensation that is sometimes known as "the helper's high."

Counselors often note that "one of the best ways to bounce back from personal problems is to help someone else with theirs" (Henderson 2012, 27). Many of the students and faculty who were interviewed had started giving back early in their lives. They looked after their younger siblings or cared for parents who suffered from physical ailments or psychological conditions, such as bipolar disorder or drug addiction. Later some volunteered to feed homeless people and refugees. A few took on the role of an institution by creating a scientific or historical museum-type exhibit to educate and entertain neighborhood children.

Connecting to the community and helping others has countless benefits in building resilience. In fact, through the environmental protective factor of community, resilient individuals may actually change their physiology. Steven G. Post (2011), professor of Preventive Medicine at SUNY Stony Brook and author of *The Hidden Gifts of Helping*, found that thoughts and actions related to helping others, when paired with genuine caring, decrease the levels of the stress hormone cortisol in the body and also increase "feel good" hormones, such as dopamine and serotonin.

He found that the caring connection system is related to the oxytocin hormone, also known as the compassion hormone. The changes in hormone levels in turn buffer stress, help to maintain a healthy heart and immune system, increase feelings of peace and joyfulness, and may even prolong life. This required helpfulness, or the ability to shift attention from "I" to "Us," can originate in childhood and often carries over into adulthood. This process is meaningful and fulfilling.

Resilient students frequently chose to major in fields directly associated with helping others and many of the resilient professors chose to teach instead of pursuing more lucrative jobs, often against their families' and friends' wishes. These individuals are aware of their keen ability to liberate themselves by liberating others.

When students connect to their communities, its members can provide a nurturing and supportive environment, an essential component for academic success (Garza et al. 2004; Lambie et al. 2003). When the community is acknowledged as an asset, schools can tap into its resources to build relationships that foster resilience among students. Neighbors, families, informal mentors, and other acquaintances become valuable and knowledgeable resources that can provide students with various forms of social capital (Lambie et al. 2004). Learning communities, service learning, and mentoring programs such as Puente are only a few of the many ways in which community colleges and other institutions of higher learning have built this bridge from the classroom out to the bigger world.

As part of an institutional Quality Enhancement Plan (QEP), El Paso Community College has built on many of its faculty connections to the larger border region and encouraged increased interaction with students. For example, the history discipline has helped develop programs that take students out into their communities, with visits to museums in the vicinity, presentations about local history, historical markers research, field trips to sites such as the Mission Trail of El Camino Real de Tierra Adentro National Historic Trail, and participation in various historical reenactments and celebrations. Engaging students in these programs includes them in experiences that are meaningful and relevant to the curriculum and serves as a potential to further their future careers.

Strong community institutions such as churches may also add to this social support network. Garza, Reyes, and Trueba (2004) write about the important role that religion plays in the social lives of Mexican Americans. They explain that when immigrants leave Mexico and cross the border into the United States, many aspects of their environment become strange and unknown, except for one—the church. They note that "Latinos are bound together by a common language and religious tradition," which have been passed down from one generation to another and therefore give meaning and purpose to their lives (14).

For many the church is a place of familiarity, where they share a common language and customs that may help to lessen the fear and anxiety of living in a new world. This and their desire to belong to an affirming group makes places of worship important supportive communities (Garza et al. 2004). The church played a vital role in fostering the resilience of Guadalupe and Valentina, who have developed the same "hunger and passion to help others in need." Guadalupe first came to the United States seeking medical treatment for her ailing ten-month-old daughter, who was diagnosed with spinal cancer and was lapsing into paralysis. An El Paso, Texas, church welcomed Guadalupe and soon began raising money and gathering the resources needed to get her infant the help she desperately needed to survive. With the support and prayers of the church community, her daughter responded well to treatment and went on to live a normal healthy life.

Valentina faced a similar crisis in her life when her husband's alcoholism spiraled out of control, which threatened to destroy their marriage and family. Right at the brink of leaving her husband, a female pastor intervened and provided them both with the counseling and guidance that kept their marriage intact. Her husband was eventually able to recover and lead a normal productive life, saving both the marriage and the family. Guadalupe and Valentina felt a great sense of gratitude toward the church and its close-knit community of members, many who were people just like them. They never forgot the role that this institution played in saving their lives and families. They both became quite active in church ministries, especially those working with children and single mothers.

Guadalupe shared the following:

> The fact that I came to this country and have been given so many opportunities motivates me to help others. My passion is to work with children who have been abused. I've seen a lot of mistreatment and injustice. Church has been my base for my spiritual foundation because through the work that we do there I have learned how much work is needed in our community. We work with people from many different places, and all walks of life and with so much need for help, *gente con mucha necesidad*. The church has no limits when it comes to serving others and that is why Valentina and I stay in college. We want to learn as much as possible so that we can provide those in need with therapy or other services.

Even though the ministry work consumes a lot of time from their busy schedules as mothers and students, they see themselves continuing no matter where life leads them. Overall, the church community provides a powerful environment for the development of both their faith and resilience.

PEDAGOGIES OF SURVIVAL

Another powerful environmental factor not discussed in the traditional literature that can play an important role in cultivating student resilience are pedagogies of survival. Pedagogies, or lessons, can be learned from cultural sources, such as everyday conversations and oral traditions. The author's grandmother, Chepa, was notorious for telling *adivinanzas* (riddles) and *dichos* (sayings) or *refranes*.

She often said, *"El que traga mas saliva come mas pinole."* The literal translation is "the person who has more saliva eats more Nahuatl pinolli flour." In a much broader sense, it means that the more knowledge, abilities, or influence a person has, the more success they will have in life. Gándara (1995) explains that these stories and sayings are a rich form of cultural capital and are directly connected to educational resilience because they "not only provide models of people who have made it, but they may engender in children a sense of hopefulness which might otherwise be absent in their lives" (54).

Simple sayings can transmit basic behaviors and values in a culture. Stories, dichos, *consejos* (advice), and cultural experience are a vital part of our pedagogies of survival, the teachings or lessons learned from our own struggles, or those of our families and ancestors. They are cultural and historical ways of knowing that can promote resilience and serve as strategies and resources. When other people, especially in an educational setting, validate them, they nurture our resilience.

Pedagogies of survival are grounded in two principles. First, the students learn to view struggle as necessary in order to achieve success in life. They have often experienced it firsthand and have witnessed how family members, such as mothers and grandmothers, have survived difficult times. The teachings lead them to create, practice, and reshape ways of knowing that are crucial to their existence. Second, persisting and prevailing over these difficulties has engendered in them *orgullo*, a deep sense of pride for being the descendents of *mujeres luchistas*, women who fight back.

This orgullo serves as a motivational force that moves the participants and their families to act. The idea that they were not "meant to survive" is the very reason why they carry on every day of their lives (Lorde 1997, 255). This orgullo is so vital to the resilience of these students that it should be validated and tapped into as a resource. Because these Mexican American students encounter challenging situations on a regular basis, drawing from and nurturing their *sabiduría* (knowledge) and orgullo strengthens their pedagogies of survival and validates their struggles.

Using a critical resilience lens allows us to extract these cultural traditions and values, traditions and values that would have been overlooked, dismissed, and certainly not validated by more conventional research (see the appendix). For example, Sofía, a twenty-eight-year-old Mexican American trilingual female, remembers growing up in a small village in rural Durango, Mexico, where life was difficult and everyone was poor. The family matriarch, her grandmother Rosario, had to stretch the family's resources to the limit. She had to be especially creative when feeding a large extended family during hard times:

> She told me one time that there was a time, or *temporada*, when breakfast was one egg for eight children. What my grandma would do was scramble, scramble, scramble and pour whatever milk she could find—like goat milk. My mom said *que hivan y se peleabán* [they would fight] over the goat. *Cada quién con su vacito hivan haber que le sacában al pobre chivo.* [Everyone with their own cup would see what they could take out of the poor goat.] Then she would scramble, scramble, scramble and would make a "huge *torta* [round cake]!" Then she would evenly divide it among them and my mom said they would eat that with tortillas and *frijoles* [beans].

Her grandmother was able to stretch the contents of one egg enough to feed her eight hungry children. In doing so, she did much more than just prepare breakfast; she modeled problem solving and creativity for her children by scrambling the egg and adding whatever was available rather than just frying it. She also made the struggle a bit of a game. While the children were busy getting in line to milk the goat, they were actually playing a role in making the meal, thereby becoming part of the solution instead of being a part of the problem. By being engaged in the process, they also forgot how hungry they were. This simple, somewhat humorous story is an example of a cultural resource that allowed Sofía to build her pedagogies of survival.

These cultural resources and how they lead to pedagogies of survival are seldom recognized as significant ways of knowing in a traditional educational setting (Campa 2013a; Moll et al. 2005). This narrative serves as a powerful lesson and caused Sofía to state, "I am proud of where I come from." She takes pride in being the granddaughter of a resilient Mexican woman from a poverty-stricken village who provided for her family in such a profound way. Grandma Rosario put the needs of the children before her own and creatively kept them adequately fed during a time of crisis. Today, when facing a challenge, Sofía's family always goes back to this story, applying it to new circumstances and passing it down to another generation. This simple tale has become an integral pedagogy of their survival.

Robert, a thirty-two-year-old bilingual Mexican American male, was also encouraged to explore his roots. As a boy, his parents sent him to spend time with his extended family in Durango, Mexico. Robert remembers that when he was thirteen years old, he attended his grandparents' fiftieth anniversary celebration, which, to his surprise, included the entire community of the village of Las Huertas:

¡*Tirarón la casa por la ventana* [They really went all out]! They had a three-
day party and it was at the ranch. Some people don't believe that they really do
party for days and days. I experienced it and that is something that I can never
forget. . . . It was immeasurable. They killed a cow and a pig and had a rodeo.

For Robert this was more than just a party; it engendered in him a sense of
belonging. The families in this community had developed strong social networks to the extent that Robert felt like he was part of something much larger
than himself. He noted that "Hey! I didn't even live there, but I felt like I did.
I mean like it was so different from here." The families in this small, traditional rural settlement shared their modest resources, such as their cows and
pigs, and engaged in activities like a *charreada*, or a Mexican-style rodeo,
and built a tight-knit community. In Las Huertas, Robert learned the importance of relationships.

Later this sense of community helped to foster Robert's pedagogies of
survival. When he first attended EPCC, Robert used his social skills to build
new relationships and create a sense of community with his teachers and
classmates. Even though he was older than many in his class and was somewhat out of touch with the younger generation, he tried to work along with
them and encourage them in their studies. Robert befriended many of his
classmates and convinced them that their classroom was a community in
which cooperation and mutual interest could help them succeed. He felt that
they were all in this together and needed to connect more with the professors,
who could ultimately help them in their future studies at a university or in a
profession.

Robert said "it's all about networking." Robert understood the importance
of social capital between the students and the faculty and its link to professional and financial opportunities. His classmates needed more concrete examples, so he explained that "I like to build a certain relationship with a
professor because what if I apply for a scholarship and I need a letter of
recommendation." This classroom engagement generated a sense of mutual
interest, reciprocity, and social trust, just as he had experienced in Las Huertas many years earlier.

Crista, a forty-one-year-old bilingual Mexican American female who was
born and raised in a modest agricultural hamlet in Durango, similar to Las
Huertas, described how her struggles had added to her pedagogies of survival. She told the story of her great grandmother's *metate*, an experience she
wrote about in a paper for an English class. She described this curved grinding stone, a common ancient utensil in the region, as being "made of volcanic
rock that comes from a mountain in the Sierra Madre Occidental, in Durango, Mexico." The metate holds great culturally significant value because her
great grandmother "used it to grind corn to make tortillas that fed Mexican
Revolutionaries."

Because grinding corn is grueling work, "the metate was handed down to the woman who was the strongest, the toughest, and hardest working." With a strong sense of pride in her voice, Crista explains that now the metate has been passed on to her. For her this ancient artifact serves as a reminder of her family's resilience because "grinding corn means that difficult times that threaten the family's survival are present." Crista is proud of being the descendent of ingenious Mexican women who possessed a strong sense of purpose in their lives that went far beyond their own immediate, individual needs. By using their many talents, these women played an important role in the Mexican Revolution, a role that has now symbolically been passed on to her.

Crista understands that this knowledge is valuable because it illustrates that there can be power in the struggles of everyday life. Even though their experiences varied, the students know that at some level their resilience is culturally and historically situated. The "metate," "huge torta," and "grandparents' anniversary" stories are teachings that serve as a foundation for their pedagogies of survival. These pedagogies reveal a deep personal knowledge of life experiences and tradition. They challenge the conventional assumption that they are somehow deficient in language, culture, and knowledge. Far from being deficient, these community college students come from backgrounds rich in oral tradition, survival skills, and heritage. They demonstrate high levels of resilience and can help us understand how students of Mexican heritage achieve success.

TEACHER QUALITIES

Another powerful environmental factor that can play an important role in cultivating student resilience is the quality of teachers and teaching, an area not commonly addressed in the traditional literature of education. At El Paso Community College, the faculty uses a variety of teaching and counseling methods to enhance students' personal and environmental protective factors, build resilience, and help them work toward their goals. High-quality teachers and their teaching methods greatly strengthen the school environment. In a sense, each teacher creates his or her own environment in each of his or her classes. The El Paso Community College faculty are particularly proud of the longstanding tradition of academic freedom, which has supported different teaching techniques, approaches, and environments over the decades.

Even though there are many factors that influence students' achievement in college, there is a substantial and growing consensus among educators that teacher quality plays a major role (Hollins and Guzman 2005). Some scholars argue that teacher quality is so significant that it transcends the influences of family, socioeconomic status, classroom size, and curriculum (Ferguson

1991; Sanders and Rivers 1996; Strauss and Sawyer 1986). Expertise contributes greatly to teacher quality.

A teacher's expertise includes knowledge of the subject matter, a deep understanding of teaching and learning, experience, and a high level of education (Cochran-Smith 2003; Darling-Hammond 2006). When these various characteristics are present in teachers, they can become part of a dynamic process that can greatly enhance student resilience. Students identify quality teaching as an intertwining or seamless blend of craft, science, and technique. This art form was found in their most passionate and committed teachers and was observed time and time again in EPCC classrooms (Bransford et al. 2005; Cochran-Smith 2003; Hollins and Guzman 2005). Along with knowledge, embodying a passionate personality is another characteristic of many of the EPCC faculty members.

Diversity is also cited as a factor. Nationally, about 79 percent of full-time college faculty are white and only 5 percent are Hispanic (National Center for Education Statistics n.d.). In addition, the majority are men. Changes in population demographics and achievement gaps among various racial and cultural groups have brought into focus the importance of diversity among educators (Hollins and Guzman 2005). EPCC far surpasses the national average levels of Hispanic faculty and is much more reflective of its student population. Students see themselves represented among the professionals at El Paso Community College, where 67 percent of the faculty members are Hispanic and 58 percent of them are women. *The Hispanic Outlook in Higher Education* (Cooper 2013) recently recognized EPCC as the community college with the largest number of Hispanic faculty in the country.

Subject Knowledge

Students particularly enjoy studying with the faculty who are knowledgeable lifelong learners because they always bring exciting new works into their classrooms. Most have advanced coursework in their fields, others have unique areas of interest, and some bring their students directly into the process of research, investigation, and writing. The students frequently commented that their best professors were much more informed and cosmopolitan than their high school teachers had been. In their EPCC classrooms, many students felt as if they had entered an entirely different world. Some faculty were pursuing or had obtained doctorates in their disciplines and participated in professional organizations. A few had written about their experiences and published works in academic journals.

Mr. Joe Old and Dr. Myshie Pagel had traveled widely and brought interesting cultural viewpoints into their classes. Mr. Lolo Mercado had an almost infinite range of personal counseling and career expertise, formally trained and supervised other counselors, and was always attending training seminars. Some simply had a scholarly air; Ms. McNiel was well connected with university faculty and had unique areas of interest. Mr. Yañez published stories of the borderlands, describing a fascinating blend of cultures in the Chicano experience. Each seemed to be able to present classroom materials in a very different and interesting way because of their varied worldly experiences. They treated the community college classroom as a laboratory, a place to experiment, and tried to draw the best out of their students.

Knowledge of Teaching and Learning

Another characteristic that the participants spoke of was the professors' knowledge of teaching and learning and the use of a variety of teaching methods. They appreciated the fact that at EPCC they were exposed to various types of teaching and learning strategies. The students believed that experiencing a diversity of teaching styles was necessary for their survival at a university and this diversity was a significant attribute of teacher quality. Because of their multicultural dispositions, these students often understood the importance of maneuvering within different types of learning environments. They experienced different types of methods, including collaborative learning and discussions. They even enjoyed the traditional lecture approach as long as the professor was energetic, had a strong base of knowledge, and made the class interesting.

Students commented that their professors' knowledge of teaching, learning, and subject matter played a vital role in their academic interests. Some students admired the fact that their teachers loved their professions and were truly excited when explaining what it was like to research an idea, write a paper or article, or uncover an interesting fact. The students preferred a sort of "Renaissance" quality in their teachers, teachers who were well read across broad areas, could communicate ideas and information in a variety of ways, and had a real intellectual curiosity. They saw this quality over and over again in the faculty whom they identified as great teachers. Guadalupe felt this way about Ms. Galindo:

> Ms. Galindo has a way of explaining very complicated concepts in simple ways. I noticed that when a student does not understand something she comes down to their level. I am sure that she could explain that same information in a sophisticated way that would wow or impress many professional people because she has so much knowledge about many topics. Instead she uses simple language and at the same time is very professional. I think this comes from the love she has for students and her profession.

Passion

Teacher personality, excitement, and passion were often cited. Robert explained:

> Some of the college professors I've had have been great! I like Mr. Joe Old because he is full of energy. I enjoy the way he teaches. He gives examples and tells interesting stories. He tells stories in such a way that make you feel like you are in the story as it is taking place. We have a lot of classroom interaction. He'll ask questions and we discuss. He is enthusiastic and goes into extreme detail. Mr. Old is passionate about English and writing because he has been all over the world. He even lived in Chicago and China and has a lot of world experience.

The next chapters feature examples of EPCC professors who possess these prime teacher qualities and explore how they develop protective factors, build resilience, and how they themselves mirror resilience.

Chapter Three

Teaching *con Respeto*

A reconception of respect in education is an approach to teaching based on the ideas of Guadalupe Valdés's (1996) work, *Con Respeto*. To teach *con respeto* is to develop a mindset and follow methods that foster resilience. It builds on the students' personal and environmental protective factors and involves a deeper level of respect and care. Most students and professors are not familiar with this term, yet they all know what *falta de respeto* (lack of respect) feels and looks like.

Respeto means caring for students in a profound way through high expectations and creative, nurturing approaches. Teaching con respeto means seeing possibility, or resilience, in students. In essence, it means holding visions of others that they cannot yet imagine for themselves (Delpit 1996). Teaching con respeto has the potential to validate the heart, mind, and the human spirit.

Knowledgeable faculty with a commitment to instruction and learning have the opportunity to teach con respeto. This approach builds social competence and creates relationships and a nurturing environment for the students. A caring relationship allows the teacher to have high expectations, pushing and driving students to reach their true potential. They become what Lisa Delpit (2012) calls a "warm demander," a teacher who firmly believes "that their students are capable of excellence" and assumes "responsibility for ensuring that their students achieve that excellence" (Ladson-Billings 1994, 23).

Teaching con respeto can take place when faculty open up their classrooms and honor the knowledge that students bring with them to these spaces. They attempt to connect with the students' worlds and share their power, allowing them to shape the curriculum and make use of their unique experiences. Professors who use this honorable approach provide their pupils opportunities for meaningful participation and foster caring relationships (Benard 2004). Many EPCC faculty who teach con respeto are humble in their approach, which is often the result of trying circumstances in their own lives that helped them develop resilience.

SOCIAL COMPETENCY THROUGH MEANINGFUL RELATIONSHIPS

The foundation of respeto is meaningful relationships. The relationships can be brief interactions in which a student experiences nurturing or guidance or long-term ones that develop over the course of their college career. In either case, these engagements can have a long-lasting impact. Many students explained that the interactions they had with their counselors and professors became meaningful, inspiring ones that created a sense of connectedness and caring. Crista's relationships with her counselors, Ms. Cristina Camacho and Mr. Lolo Mercado, were forms of connected knowing that are grounded in caring (Belenky et al. 1986). These counselors welcomed students into the college as if it were their home, helping them find their way and becoming both their friends and mentors. Crista noted that

> the attitude and motivation that they have is contagious. I think that people that go above and beyond make the college look good and they make the experience for the student a positive one. I feel that that is the beginning of the student being successful. I strongly feel that attitude is important. The helpful and caring attitude helps to motivate you to be here. I mean you actually want to be here.

Valenzuela (1999) explains that this interaction between students and teachers is crucial to learning and that this authentic care is parallel to the broader Mexican definition of *educación*, "a model of schooling premised on respectful, caring relationships" (61). For Crista, this engagement provided her with inspiration that enhanced her *orgullo*, or her strong sense of pride. More importantly, as Mexican American professionals, Ms. Camacho and Mr. Mercado also served as role models and helped Crista build social competency and connect with the community beyond EPCC. They promote EPCC as a friendly, accessible institution in which students feel comfortable, are encouraged, and can cultivate their resilience.

Even when Crista was not taking classes, she still made an effort to be a part of the college. She kept in contact with some of the professors who had been particularly supportive and continued to be involved in activities sponsored by EPCC. Mr. Leon Blevins, a government professor, engages his students in off-campus activities such as seminars, debates, or public gatherings. Even though Crista was no longer enrolled in his classes, she still participated in some of the community events that Mr. Blevins sponsored or promoted. Crista enthusiastically recalls one encounter:

> One time I saw him at the College's administrative building. He was there because he too had created a poem. We got out of there and we were so happy to see each other that we went to a coffee shop. We had coffee and talked for a long time. It was so great to be there with my professor! He is so sweet and I have a lot of respect for him. I got home at 9:30 PM and my husband said, "What took you so long?" "Guess who I saw? You are going to be so jealous! I saw Mr. Blevins and we went and had coffee!"

Many of these students "have been underserved and invalidated in the past" (Rendón 2002, 655). At EPCC, the faculty's role in educación, building nurturing connections and social competence, helps the students feel at ease in the college environment and enhances their academic resilience.

Angel had a similar experience with an EPCC counselor who took on a special interest in him and steered him toward an important remedial program under Title V:

> The purpose was to refresh my memory. I didn't want to get placed into remedial courses. I did not want to take classes that I would not get credit for. So I took that course. It was through the Plato Program. I was able to do it online from my house. I took the courses and took a placement test and scored really well on it. That allowed me to take college level courses.

As a nontraditional student returning to school, Angel needed direction and guidance. In her studies of community colleges, Rendón (1994) found that these nontraditional students "do not perceive involvement as *them* taking the initiative," but "rather as others taking an active role in assisting them" (44). Therefore nontraditional college students "benefit substantially from direct, sustained, and genuinely supportive (non-patronizing) academic and interpersonal validation" (Rendón 2002, 663).

Because the counselor who helped Angel played an active role in gathering information about his background, she was able to determine that he had been out of the college sphere for more than ten years, needed some additional assessment, and could benefit from programs such as those offered through Title V. This "direct" action provided Angel with knowledge that served as a bridge, a pathway across multiple barriers, thus bolstering his resilience. This brief social encounter signaled something much bigger to Angel: that EPCC took an interest in his needs. He was surprised how counselors and professors frequently took the lead and provided him with specific guidance and assistance.

These social relationships with students are generally fluid and can extend beyond the classroom and other campus settings. Over time, the commitment of the counselor or teacher to the student often becomes reciprocal. As Ladson-Billings (1994) describes it, they develop "a greater commitment to learning because of their commitment to their teachers [and counselors]" (125). Sofía found that as she was encouraged to explore her skills and strengths, she became more engaged with the teachers who nurtured her, demanded more from her, and gently pushed her to her limits. She stated that "At first you think, 'I'm scared. I don't want to do that. I'm not going to do it right!' But then they give you feedback and tell you, 'You did a good job!' And that is very important." Simple reinforcement can raise the bar and motivate a student further.

Ms. Elizabeth Carrillo is an example of a professor who is a warm demander and teaches con respeto. One of the often-cited teacher qualities is the ability to connect with the students' worlds. Sofía emphasized how important it was for professors to "make it real." For her, a Mexican American female, "making it real" meant discussing topics related to racism, classism, sexism, and other issues that she and her family had experienced. It also meant that her struggles and those of other people counted as knowledge. Sofía describes how some of her professors taught in ways that validated subjective forms of knowledge and pushed the students farther in their thinking (Belenky et al. 1986):

> I've been really lucky because I've had great teachers. My English teacher, Ms. Carrillo was awesome! She kept me interested! She had discussions in class. She would say, "Okay you guys were supposed to read such and such short story. What did you guys think about it?" Or she would ask us other questions. I would be like, "I read the stories! I know the answer (enthusiastic voice)!" She kept it really interesting because she picked different stories about racism, poverty, and culture. She picked issues that are happening now, and I think that is what is interesting. She would make it real or a part of reality. I really enjoyed the open discussions.

Ms. Carrillo selected readings and gave her students projects that "demanded" them to, as Delpit (2006) describes, "think critically about what they were learning and about the world at large" (223). Sofía shared the discomfort that she was experiencing at the beginning of the semester and asked for assistance from the author, her Education 1300 professor at the time. Sofía explained that Ms. Carrillo had asked her to write a research paper critiquing and analyzing a short story about an African American female and her struggles:

> I think it was in my English class when I thought, "Oh I'm not going to be able to do this" because she made it sound like it was going to be the hardest thing. The first day she based it on—you need to turn in a good research paper and if you don't have a good research paper you're not going to have a good time. So then I thought, "It's got to be the greatest work." The whole semester I strug-

gled with the research paper. But then I had a few people along the way that helped me out, like you. I kept trying and trying and giving her draft after draft. I told myself, "I have to do it right." So I always asked her questions and went to the writing center. I don't know how many times I went. I also got extra credit for going so that was more of a reason why I was going. I think that class was the one that really opened my eyes. Now I notice that when I write, ¡*Hay me salio bonito* [It comes out beautiful]!

Ms. Carrillo gently nudged Sofía along, warmly demanding progress and results, and made sure that her work truly did become beautiful.

FACULTY TEACHING CON RESPETO

Teaching con respeto allows the faculty to share power, develop students' critical thinking skills, have high expectations, and create a stimulating environment. In the broader sense of educación, teachers are able to be warm demanders, validate knowledge and experiences, engage, develop relationships, and build resilience.

Personal experience can be the thread that draws the mind, body, and soul together. It is an important aspect of knowledge and empowerment and is intricately connected to learning and teaching. The knowledge that students bring to the classroom can be extremely valuable, and when teachers make use of this knowledge, they are able to connect the abstract academic world directly to the world of the student. They often have detailed, complex knowledge of their own families and communities, which can be used to bolster their understanding of greater social, political, economic, or cultural changes underway.

Using personal experience in the classroom to empower students is a challenging endeavor. The teacher must learn about the student's world and incorporate their knowledge into the coursework. Mr. Joe Old, English professor and former faculty adviser of the *Tejano Tribune* (EPCC's student newspaper), understood this paradigm well and used his creativity to learn more about his students' experiences outside of the classroom and how to connect his teaching to their world. He possessed many of the key teacher qualities: expertise, knowledge of content and learning, passion, and high expectations. He clearly teaches his students con respeto.

Joe Old developed an inquiry project in which students studied their own neighborhood and tried to answer the questions that a real estate agent might be presented with when selling a property. First, the students were asked to take a leisurely walk around their community and pen down a few basic notes on what they observed. What was their first impression? What caught their eye for the first time?

They researched general data about the area. When was it developed? How old are the houses? How many people live there? Where do they work? Then they were asked to conduct personal interviews and gather information about schools, businesses, places of employment, services, and facilities. After the initial research, students were asked to write about their experiences and summarize and highlight what they learned about their neighborhood.

Not only did Mr. Old and his class learn about many unique communities, but the students were often shocked by what they discovered. Some learned that their house was part of an important era in the development of the city, the arrival of the railroad, the Mexican Revolution, or the construction of Interstate 10. Some found that their neighborhoods had formal names they had never heard of.

A few students learned that their neighborhood was a hard sell; it had traditionally low incomes, many dilapidated buildings, or poorly rated schools (schools that they had attended)! Whatever the results, it sure stirred their imaginations and instilled in them a new interest regarding their surroundings. Mr. Old had turned a routine classroom assignment into a means of empowering his pupils and helping them learn that they and their families were really a part of something much bigger.

Mr. Old also understood the power of the narrative and assigned writing projects that told a story. He asked students to find an interesting family example of success or failure, a story told among relatives or maybe one that had been kept a secret. Students could write "a sad tale or a tragic story, one that is somehow always present in people's lives even though it's not told very often." It could also be "inspiring . . . or one told as a warning." Mr. Old proudly claims that "this was by far the most fun assignment" because it produced amazing, incredible tales.

One female student wrote about her husband, the youngest of six children. After his parents died, the oldest child seized most of the family's property and left the other siblings without any inheritance. After some extensive digging, a few people began to talk. It turned out that much of the "inheritance" had been obtained through fraud. With the information gathered for Mr. Old's project, the other siblings were able to recover some of the property.

It seems like almost every family has a dark side. Another female student told a shocking story she had heard about her great grandmother's marriage in Old Mexico. After a beautiful wedding and a joyous reception, the young couple had bid adieu to their friends and family and rode off into the sunset to begin their new life. But later it was discovered that the young bride and her family had been duped. She was essentially kidnapped when the husband took his new wife off to an isolated ranch, tied her up, abused her, and put her to work in the fields as a slave.

Joe Old used students' knowledge to build curriculum and created meaningful assignments that honored their own experiences and their culture. In doing so, he validated their pedagogies of survival. He understood that his students led interesting lives:

> Lucy, a former student and actress who had starred in Mexican television programs, said that we make the mistake of saying "out in the real world" when we talk about our environment being artificial. It's only artificial in one sense. These students walk right out of reality into our classes, and they often have amazing lives that lead to amazing stories.

A resilient teacher can recognize and develop resilience in his or her students. A few conversations with Mr. Old revealed that he himself had a story of his own and brought many adventurous, diverse, and worldly experiences to the classroom.

Joe was a Peace Corps volunteer who taught history and English in Ethiopia. He served in the U.S. Air Force during the Vietnam War and was among the earliest groups of second lieutenants stationed in Thailand. He maintained F-105 jets, the famous aircraft that led bombing raids in Vietnam. Joe's literary talents were recognized by his colonel, the chief of maintenance, who soon put him to work on routine office memos, letters, and directives.

He was told that when he was not servicing aircrafts, his "job here is to make sure that every piece of paper that goes out of here with my name on it is perfect, no mistakes." The colonel said, "I want you to come in here every morning and check everything that requires my signature, make sure that I'm not signing anything with a mistake in it."

Joe was granted permission to use the library at Garrett Air Force Base in order to comply with his colonel's request. He used to spend hours reading about Chinese history and contemplating the U.S. dilemma in Vietnam. After leaving the Air Force, Joe Old pursued a doctorate in Chinese history at the University of Illinois and moved to China for eighteen months to improve his fluency in the language. Academic positions in Chinese history were rare in 1977, so instead he earned a master's degree in Journalism and went to work for a famous old wire service, the City News Bureau of Chicago.

Joe experienced a daily rush of adrenaline as he confronted whatever the world threw at him each day. "You could be out on the street covering a murder and get a call from the city desk saying that IBM is having a news conference at the best hotel in downtown. Get there by three o'clock! In minutes you would go from the poorest area where there is violence to a fancy hotel with people in suits and business attire." Not knowing what story he would be writing about next kept Joe alert and on his feet:

It was really, really life-changing because you had to learn how to interview anybody and everybody. I got stuck on an elevator one time with George Bush Sr. and Jesse Jackson at the same time. I was caught off guard. I wanted to ask George Bush a question but couldn't quite formulate it and so I stammered as I was riding down the elevator. By the time I got to the bottom floor, he said, "Well that's just too complex," and walked off. Even though I did not get my answer it was great to have the opportunity.

Professor Old brings all of this energetic intellect and knowledge to the classroom, which are prime teacher qualities. He shares power with his students and honors their knowledge by exploring the stories of their families and communities.

Robert, a former student, raves about Joe Old's love for reading, writing, history, philosophy, and politics. He describes how he has a unique ability to engage students in meaningful ways and how he motivated and inspired him to learn more. Robert's background and lack of academic role models helped him forge a connection with Mr. Old. The only child of two immigrant parents, Robert had a comfortable upbringing and benefited from his parents' strong ties to their families in Mexico.

As a child, he spent many holidays and summers in Las Huertas, a small town in Durango, where he experienced living in a traditional rural village. In his teens, he embarked on one of the great adventures of his life, traveling alone on the train through Mexico, immersing himself in the world of Las Huertas and becoming well grounded in his heritage and culture.

Robert's father had many traditional Mexican *macho* attitudes that sometimes made him uncomfortable. He related more to an uncle, whom he saw as having a more open and tender side. Both men served as influential role models for Robert. He describes them both as hardworking, self-sufficient men who started out as immigrants and built successful businesses and enterprises both in the United States and in Mexico. His father worked at a dairy because of his ranching background in Mexico and eventually established a small business that sold milk and dairy products. He also bought older appliances, refurbished them, and opened a secondhand store across the border in Ciudad Juárez.

As a young man, Robert attended school, but like many of his friends, he did not consider it "cool" to be smart. His father and uncle encouraged him to pursue sports, so he followed the more traditional role of an athlete throughout middle school and high school. Because he was a good athlete and an important member of the school's teams, Robert was never influenced much academically or intellectually by his teachers or counselors. Instead he was a celebrity at school and reveled in the lively social scene. His teachers were often lenient with his work and allowed him to coast through the years and graduate. After completing high school, Robert enrolled at EPCC but found that his lack of preparation was a great obstacle. Discouraged, he left college and followed another "manly" pursuit instead: a career in the military.

Robert served in the Navy as a translator. This gave him the opportunity to travel extensively, making acquaintances from different parts of Latin America. After leaving the military, Robert returned home and reenrolled at El Paso Community College. This time he brought with him many years of experience, but he still lacked some basic academic skills. It took him several semesters to rebuild his GPA. In the process, he became reacquainted with a high school friend who was now a community college professor.

Their friendship, and the encouragement provided by Mr. Old, instilled new academic interests in Robert, and he now sees being scholarly as a positive attribute. Mr. Old served as a new mirror and role model for him. Robert is now interested in pursuing a career in education, perhaps becoming a counselor in order to guide other Mexican American students.

Classroom observations revealed what students often described. Mr. Old integrated history and philosophy into his classes and taught English in a dramatic narrative style with constant references and examples from the present day. Mr. Old walked around the room and conveyed enthusiasm through his thunderous voice and excited gestures. He used analytical exercises to teach literature and writing. He emphasized social justice issues, urging his students to critically review and analyze the deeper meaning of the texts. Professor Old taught his classes con respeto, valuing students' knowledge and always having high expectations.

For twenty years, Joe Old also brought his fiery journalistic style to the EPCC student newspaper, the *Tejano Tribune*. His student editors and reporters truly learned about relationships of power and were encouraged to dig deep into the news, raise interesting questions, and not be intimidated, even in the heat of scandals. Rather than a public relations piece for athletic programs, reporting awards, or simply recounting day-to-day registration and enrollment figures, the student paper was filled with investigative pieces and controversial issues. Today, everyone remembers when Joe Old was the advisor for the student newspaper and how, throughout the college, people anxiously awaited for the latest issue to be published.

Joe Old's varied background allowed him to go even further by combining his knowledge of English, students in the borderlands, and the use of language as a form of social and cultural capital. His teaching experience and his desire to help Spanish-speaking students improve their communicative skills in English led him to co-author a work with fellow EPCC English professor and close friend Ted Johnston. Together they wrote a textbook, *English Beyond the Basics: A Handbook for Spanish Speakers*. Then in 2011 they published a revised edition, *Navigating from Spanish to English*.

How was this man from a dusty West Texas town able to make some of his worldly experiences mesh with students' knowledge and come alive in a community college classroom? In Parker Palmer's (1998) words, "we teach who we are." So who is Joe Old? Joe Old's story is not much different than mine or those of our students:

> Our biggest problem is that we were very poor. It was difficult. We lived in Plainview when I was in the 5th and 6th grades, and my dad lived in Lubbock. My mother and dad were divorced. Then he started a little company, a pest control company in Lubbock. He finally convinced us to come to Lubbock, so they got re-married. It was a seasonal business. In the spring, when the bugs start coming out, that's when people call and they call through the summer. Then from November to April, it was really tough, and I remember that one year from Thanksgiving to Christmas, my dad's company made a total of fourteen dollars and fifty cents. We sprayed one house for bugs. Growing up was difficult.

One winter, the plumbing in their apartment froze and there was no money to fix it. So for the next three months, Joe and his family had to use the bathroom at the Phillips 66 service station around the corner. As a result, his mother sank into a deep depression and ten-year-old Joe avoided much of the stress by sleeping to alleviate his fears. Monday became Joe's favorite day of the week because he could return to school, where he was considered a smart kid and was rewarded for doing homework and being a good student.

I had similar experiences when growing up in Ciudad Juárez. A difficult, chaotic personal life was often balanced by teachers who helped to cultivate our resilience. They provided positive and encouraging feedback and support that permitted us to feel some agency and exercise a bit of control over our lives. Teachers created experiences that gave meaning and meaning translated into a larger sense of purpose and desire to teach others. This allowed people like me and Joe Old to find possibility, or resilience, in EPCC students and hold visions of others that they cannot yet imagine for themselves (Delpit 1996).

A Worldly Professor

Dr. Myshie Pagel is a tall, blue-eyed woman with blondish-gray hair and a strong, energetic, worldly air. She is white, but many students are surprised to learn that she is Hispanic, raised in a bilingual home by a mother of Chilean descent. Myshie's grandparents were missionaries in South America. Her father and mother met, fell in love, and married while living in Chile. Through her parents, Myshie became fluent in Spanish and developed a multicultural worldview of great depth. Later she and her husband carried on with the family's missionary work. This blending of cultures became a motivating force in Myshie's life as she and her husband traveled the world, broadening their horizons even further.

Her first son was born while she was conducting field studies in North Africa. She realized that she loved to "travel and to live cross-culturally," so she pursued a career as a teacher and helped others learn English as their second language. She wants students to understand complexity, to look under the surface to a place that can lead to many interesting discoveries:

> I find that most students make a lot of assumptions about me when they first see me . . . so in class, we talk about stereotypes and assumptions to make it real. I say, "Okay what did you think about me? What were the assumptions you made about me when you first came into class?" And there's silence. Once you get them going they do the whole list. "It's okay to talk about this. You assumed I was white and that means I'm rich, right? That I only speak one language, that I was born here, and this is where I have lived all my life, and on and on." I say "Okay, well this is who I am." I start telling them, and they are shocked.

Dr. Pagel thinks it is her responsibility to deconstruct stereotypes and help students expand their thinking. She wants them to learn that "whiteness has many variations" and dimensions. When I asked why this was important, Myshie explained that while she was growing up, her mother did not have a college degree, but her father was always learning and encouraged her to do the same. They helped her develop an inquisitive mind, and she wants the same for her students. "I want them to transfer the knowledge from the classroom to other areas of their life—and not just learn ideas and skills in isolation."

When the students have difficulty building connections, she asks herself, "Why?" Myshie's students usually have very busy, challenging lives. They often have low incomes, kids at home, and many household responsibilities. Because of cultural issues such as machismo, women particularly have to answer to their families about going to college or becoming well versed in English. She is often amazed at how complex and confrontational their lives are and therefore treats class time as a precious commodity, one of the few times they can focus solely on a problem or an issue. Dr. Pagel is determined to help students discover knowledge that is both empowering and meaningful, knowledge that allows them to overcome many of their challenges, prevail, and transform their lives.

Her students are very lucky because Myshie has many prominent teacher qualities. She has a great knowledge of many academic fields, has received recognition for her teaching, and, along with impressive credentials, has a firm scholarly background. Dr. Pagel was once described by a former student as a media correspondent "who knew everything." Many of the students are humble and unassuming, so over the years she has found that teaching con respeto allows her to build nurturing relations with them, enhance their social competency, and, as a warm demander, maintain high expectations.

Valentina and Guadalupe found her to be immeasurably helpful:

Valentina: The only reason we survived English 1301 is because Ms. Pagel had prepared us so well in our ESL writing courses. It was a drastic change. For example, when we would make a written mistake, Ms. Pagel would identify it, and it was important for her that we understood why we had made that error. So we would correct it and then this would help us to understand why we had made the grammatical error. Sometimes she would place an "X" across it and other times she would tell us other words that could be used instead. This way, we had choices and knew what words to use next time.

Guadalupe: When we would give Ms. Pagel an essay she would always explain to us in great detail what type of essay she wanted us to write. If it was a compare and contrast essay she would show us examples and we would look at the textbook and it would explain what type of transitions we needed to write.

Valentina: Ms. Pagel also taught us how to use MLA. Even our English teacher said, "You can't speak the language well but you sure can write it."

Just like an airplane needs great power and energy to lift itself off the runway, students need professors to push them to their full potential, even if it triggers discomfort. Part of Sofía's academic frustration was due to the fact that she was asked to complete a project that required her to go above and beyond the knowledge that she already had.

Sofía, Guadalupe, and Valentina quickly became aware that Ms. Carrillo and Dr. Pagel had very high standards and expected a lot from them and the other students. Dr. Pagel taught Guadalupe and Valentina everything from putting together a complete sentence or paragraph to using MLA style proficiently. In doing this, Dr. Pagel added one more layer to Guadalupe's and Valentina's resilience. In essence, she lifted these students off the ground and gently helped them reach their cruising altitude.

She and other faculty used the classroom as an environmental protective factor by teaching the students skills that helped them become autonomous and competent problem solvers. The stronger social connections with students allowed the teachers to expect and receive higher quality work. This is evident when Sofía states that now when she writes, her writing "comes out beautiful!" and when Valentina said proudly, "When I first started college I did not even know how to turn on a computer. *Gracias* Dr. Pagel!" Guadalupe said, "I often tell myself, 'Wow! Look at everything I have learned!'"

Challenging Traditional Beliefs

Myshie Pagel works closely with Rose Galindo, a petite, four-foot-nine, caramel-colored professor who has dark, penetrating eyes that command immediate attention. She is described by her students as energetic, spirited, compassionate, and committed. Rose and Myshie assign readings that are inspiring and portray various historical and contemporary figures who have struggled immensely but have prevailed; people who are truly resilient.

In their writing and reading ESL classes, they have read, analyzed, discussed, and written about Thomas Jefferson's "Declaration of Independence," Frederick Douglass's fiery 1842 speech "What to the Slave Is the Fourth of July?" and the "Letter from the Birmingham Jail" penned by Dr. Martin Luther King Jr. in 1963, during one of his darkest hours. The students also created photo stories to document their personal histories of struggle, resilience, and strength. Teaching con respeto, building on the students' knowledge and challenging them to think broadly and critically, are typical of the work these professors directly engage in.

Teaching con respeto provides a nurturing environment in which the student is challenged but comfortable. Rose Galindo's personal educational experiences left her somewhat traumatized, unable to function well in school and extremely unsure of her abilities and talents. Her parents came to the United States from a small rural area of Mexico and, although they were not formally educated, they were hard workers. Her father toiled as a butcher in a meat market and Mrs. Galindo was a stay-at-home mom who raised Rose and her two brothers.

The family was supportive and optimistic but was unable to help Rose much with her education. When she was in kindergarten, her parents decided to move to the east side of El Paso, where the "good schools" were located. The all-white neighborhood was on the edge of the city, and everything past their house was open desert. Rose, her father, mother, and two brothers were completely isolated. They did not speak any English and did not know a single soul in their community. School made things worse. She was placed with a teacher who spoke Spanish, Mrs. Lopez.

The school did not offer bilingual instruction and "half of the time I did not know what was going on. I kept falling behind." She spent most of the time in tutoring or remediation and was constantly being tested. Rose was placed in Ms. Howl's third-grade class, where her experiences only got worse. "I was an extremely quiet eight-year-old girl who never really said much. I was too scared to speak."

Rose felt that maybe Ms. Howl "had it in for her" and went out of her way to make her feel uncomfortable. Once Ms. Howl handed Rose a Mexican flag and asked her to come to the front of the class. She asked Rose to explain to everyone that she was Mexican. She remembers being very confused and thinking "I was born in Chicago. Maybe Chicago is in Mexico?" Friday spelling tests were the worst. In an awkward, anglicized voice, Ms. Howl would say "ROSELEA now bring your words up front and spell them out loud to the class."

To this day, Rose still remembers the exact location of her rickety little desk in the back of the room and the long, seemingly endless walk to the front of the class. Instead of the third-grade vocabulary that her classmates were learning, Rose was still struggling with a first-grade workbook.

There is nothing that elementary kids enjoy more than when a classmate is humiliated by their teacher, and each Friday the mob looked forward to the gory spectacle. Rose became extremely nervous, felt pains in her upper stomach, and one more time failed to spell the words correctly. Ms. Howl gave her a passing grade but explained that "you really failed but I just feel sorry for you." Her parents were given a grim prognosis; Rose Galindo had difficulty learning and was warned that she would not make it through the public schools. However, Rose did persevere, survive, and was able to graduate from high school.

Rose's years in elementary school had left a very bitter taste in her mouth and soured her on her educational experience. She enrolled at El Paso Community College but still felt out of place:

> First of all, I think that I went to the community college because I was afraid of the university. I don't think that I was ready for the university and I would tell people, "It's too far and I don't have a car." But that was a lie. I really felt deficient as a student and not ready. I was scared to death. I think that for the most part that is how a large number of our students feel. Can I do this? I think instructors should understand that. That is the biggest fear our students come with. Students ask, "Am I college material?" Instructors should be able to say, "Yes you are and this is what it takes!" Right?

After completing her basic coursework at EPCC, she transferred to the University of Texas at El Paso, worked part-time at a small greeting card store, and decided to major in Speech Pathology.

One day, an incident at the card store changed her mindset and sent her off on an entirely new direction in life. A black gentleman in his late fifties, nicely dressed in dark pants, blue pinstripes, and a button-up shirt, entered the store looking for a card for a new "significant other" in his life. Rose led him to a selection of cards but before she could leave, the man asked, "Ma'am, which one would you like?"

She explained that "it's not about what I like but about what you want to say. It's a personal thing. It has to come from you." The man then confessed that he could not read and Rose, somewhat shocked, offered to read a few cards for him and helped him pick the right one. Weeks went by but she could not get this moment out of her mind. She wondered what life would be like for adults who could not read or write. Her heart went out to this gentle-man and other people who were illiterate, so she started tutoring at El Paso Community College. A few months later, she was offered a teaching job in the reading lab.

In recent years, Rose Galindo has worked closely with Myshie Pagel in developing creative curriculum for their ESL students. Professors Galindo and Pagel create assignments that challenge students' ways of thinking and put them in the sometimes uncomfortable position of "critically" assessing a mainstream idea. For example, a common misconception among Hispanic students at EPCC is that racism is a unique, deeply rooted American ideology and that white Anglos have used color to oppress and sometimes erase the paths of African Americans in this country throughout history. To look at this history more critically and to place racism in a much larger, cultural context, the two professors studied and then assigned to their students "revisionist" works.

To illustrate this, their classes read segments of Jameelah S. Muham-mad's work in *No Longer Visible: Afro Latin Americans Today* (1995). The rather obscure book builds off of revisionist research of the late twentieth century. It argues that race dominated centuries of colonial and independent rule in Latin American countries and produced deep social divisions and traditions that remain common today.

The reading introduced topics, such as the Mexican government's *blanca-miento* (whitening) and other efforts to "improve the race" by diluting Indian and African ancestry through racial mixing. Students watched segments of the award-winning 2011 PBS series *Black in Latin America* by Henry Louis Gates Jr. to learn about the contributions of Afro-Mexicans and the lingering African past throughout the region. Gates vividly describes how Gaspar Yan-ga, an African who escaped servitude in the state of Veracruz, led one of the first slave rebellions and founded the first free black town in the Americas.

More than half a million African slaves were brought to Mexico and Peru, more than the number transported to the United States, and entire regions of the countries based their development and history on the slave trade. During the nineteenth century, the population was enumerated by *castas*, or castes, identifying the specific racial makeup of individuals. The program traced the lives of many prominent Mexicans of African descent, such as Vicente Guer-rero, who officially abolished slavery in 1829, and José María Morelos y Pavón, the revolutionary military commander who led the early nineteenth-century independence movement. During the program, many of the students were baffled, as this was the first time they had ever heard of the African world of Mexico.

Ms. Galindo and Dr. Pagel then led a class discussion that was riveting. They wanted the writings and videos to challenge the students' critical think-ing skills, but also wanted to respect their often emotional and sometimes defensive reactions. Some of the students were shocked that their Mexican academies and primary schools had neglected to teach them anything about the black Latin history, as if it did not exist. Juana said, "I went to an elementary school in Juárez and my teachers did not teach me this."

They commented on seemingly innocent, derogatory terms commonly used throughout the country that refer to darkness. These, such as *Mi negrita* or *Juana la Cubana*, now appeared to have racial overtones. Some wondered if their own round-shaped eyes, full lips, or mocha-colored skin might be the result of African ancestry.

Why do Mexicans continue to, as Gates described it, "keep their black grandmas in the closet?" Ms. Galindo and Dr. Pagel posed questions to guide the discussion and listened attentively. This was the students' discussion and even controversial comments needed to be accepted so that the dialog was not stifled. Every once in a while they responded with "hum, that is interesting" or "I had not thought of it that way." They asked why Mexico would have so many castas to delineate racial ancestry, especially African. Their questions included, "Why are the Mexican soap stars, journalists, and political figures so fair-skinned?"

A challenge to mainstream ideas can be risky, even when it is grounded in solid scholarly sources. By this point in the semester, Ms. Galindo and Dr. Pagel had built a concrete foundation of respeto. The students trusted these teachers, so they were comfortable expressing their ideas, but some chose to do so privately after class. A small group followed Dr. Pagel to her office where they confided that they thought the readings and videos were a huge exaggeration based on lies.

The classroom experience was a bit unnerving, but Ms. Galindo and Dr. Pagel thought that the discussion had gone well and that the student responses were fairly typical. They had simply allowed the materials to challenge the students' ideas and had led them through an uncomfortable discussion. Ms. Galindo explained that "students should not come to college to be comfortable. Education should shake your core beliefs and should tell you why we throw stones" (referring to the famous 1948 Shirley Jackson short story "The Lottery").

Following the class discussion and student interviews, it was clear that these two professors had been pedagogically successful in fostering academic and intellectual resilience. The author was a bit "shaken" and felt a bump in her own Richter scale. It raised new questions, and she now wondered where her own thick, coarse, curly head of hair had originated.

How did Ms. Rose Galindo and Dr. Myshie Pagel transform a reading and writing ESL learning community into a course on critical analysis, problem solving, self-empowerment, and social awareness—all protective factors of resilience? Ms. Galindo and Dr. Pagel have been collaborating for the past five years and following the basic principles of teaching con respeto. They look at themselves as students rather than "experts." Therefore they explore learning from within and outside of their fields through conferences and memberships in organizations, list serves, blogs, and study groups. They are avid readers, share ideas, and provide each other with honest feedback.

Dr. Pagel and Ms. Galindo enthusiastically plan and collaborate regularly for hours at length during the semester. They review new approaches and assignments and critique many that they have tried in their classes. Both mentioned that the trust they had built enabled them to tell each other "when things were not working."

While pedagogy and knowledge are important, the mindset of these professors is their most remarkable teacher quality. Mr. Joe Old, Dr. Myshie Pagel, and Ms. Rose Galindo have a profound level of respect and care for their students and their backgrounds. This allows them to help build social competency, honor the students' knowledge, and share power in the classroom. They help students answer basic questions about their identity, heritage, and community. Through high expectations and opportunities for meaningful engagement, they teach con respeto and build resilience among students.

Chapter Four

Validation

First-year experience courses are filled with excited, optimistic students who are new to the entire world of college. They hope to meet new people, establish friendships, broaden their horizons, and move closer to pursuing their goals and aspirations. While the transition is filled with hope and promise, it can also bring a great sense of anxiety, and in some cases fear and rejection. Laura Rendón, professor of Higher Education at the University of Texas at San Antonio and a nationally acclaimed expert on Hispanics and the first-year experience, reminds us that anxiety and fear are often triggered by the fact that "many students of color come from worlds removed from academics—ethnic and racial enclaves, housing projects, barrios, or reservations where few have completed college" (Rendón et al. 2004, 37).

This is certainly the case for many of the students at El Paso Community College, who are often the first in their family to attend college, are Spanish speakers in the process of learning English, have been out of school for some time, and come from families with limited resources and knowledge about higher education.

According to Rendón, many of these students—especially nontraditional community college students—lack validation, a process that she describes as an "enabling, confirming, and supportive [one]" (2004, 42). Their life experiences have not proven or confirmed that they are college bound or can be a part of the process of higher education. Instead they have had "invalid" experiences in which they have been marginalized, typecast, or ignored. They tend to slip into the background and feel that maybe the academic world is not really a place where they belong. In public schools, they may have been tracked into vocational programs rather than tutored and mentored to prepare for college. They may have been asked to select a career or choose majors or fields that they knew little about.

Some of these experiences have been invalidating. Their day-to-day problems confirm this worldview. The world seems beyond their control and attending college appears remote or inaccessible. They attribute the loss of a job to a hostile boss or to bad luck. They get distracted by and overwhelmed with limited financial resources to pay their bills, struggle with learning a new language while raising a family, or coping with the death of a loved one. Once enrolled, they often find the process intimidating, a nameless, faceless college experience. They are a registration number, always at the end of the line in a crowd, overlooked, and not asked to participate.

Even if they survive the initial ordeal, they may simply be pushed, once again, into fields of study or careers that may or may not be the best for them. The boys will study business and the girls will train to be elementary school teachers. Brooks (2015) describes this as a process in which one loses faith in progress; they doubt whether input leads to predictable output. Therefore an important step in the validation process is to structure experiences that build the students' confidence, create a new perspective through which they can control their destiny, and help them develop a sense of autonomy.

Nontraditional students, and particularly students of color, have difficulty building connections and finding guidance in college. So professors, counselors, and staff need to take measures to ensure that they are validated so that they can achieve academic success. This can be done by structuring learning and engaging students in ways that allow them to see themselves as capable, lifelong learners. Students can then reassess and redirect themselves and set off on a pathway to success. How can an institution "validate" a student's experiences? First-year experience courses, learning communities, and focused academic and personal counseling can go a long way in validating Mexican American community college students, getting them off to a good start.

THE FIRST-YEAR EXPERIENCE COURSE

Overall, community college students are more likely to become discouraged and, as noted before, the first year in college is "especially significant for certain populations: students of color, nontraditional students, first-generation college students, low-income students, under-prepared students, and those for whom English is a second language" (Anderson 2004, 77). Because community colleges draw heavily from these populations, validating these students can be far more important than validating those at traditional four-year institutions, especially as the first-year experience course is often seen as a frivolous or an unnecessary class by many of the students who need it the most. EPCC's first-year experience course, Education 1300, can be particularly useful in assessing students' personalities, skills, and abilities, which can help them understand that these can be useful assets in becoming a successful student and developing a strategy for lifelong learning. In other words, it can validate students and help them build resilience.

Primary college skills, such as taking notes, time management, and test taking, are essential in most fields of study, so they are important components of the curriculum of the course. In addition, students work with library resources, technology, research, and writing projects. Students can explore various careers and research career trends, programs of study, and opportunities for employment. They can gather information about salaries, training opportunities, future prospects in the field they are interested in, and graduate studies.

But a first-year experience course can also bring out untapped and undeveloped skills and experiences in areas that are less obvious or even unknown to the student. They can use the course to explore new areas and map out new pathways.

Sometimes working in construction during a summer break creates some curiosity about building design and architecture. Or maybe a family financial crisis reveals a student's aptitude for money management, budgeting, or long-term strategizing. An opportunity to do a class presentation helps hidden dramatic skills or speaking abilities become more obvious and effective. Or perhaps a classroom exercise, such as working with personality or career assessments, reveals to a student that he or she has interests or aptitudes that the student was never aware of.

Brooklyn learned that she had an inquiring scientific mind and was able to develop this into a career in psychology. Amanda's ability to solve some of her financial problems in order to attend a college of her choice was revealed in an Education 1300 class, in which she studied money management and found that she had a knack for creative budgeting and savings. In all of these cases, an aptitude was revealed and validated through exploration.

An assessment of learning styles can further help in the process. A student may realize for the first time that he or she is a kinesthetic learner and that he or she responds much better to, and retains better from, hands-on approaches and physical activities. This can be a surprising revelation, one that leads the student in an entirely new direction when confronting difficult or complicated course materials.

The process can help students understand new ideas and concepts, allowing them to closely examine themselves and their own lives and begin a journey of personal and career development. Students are asked to integrate and apply learning, motivation, and meta-cognitive theories in order to foster academic success. Counseling, psychology, career exploration, and critical thinking are all part of the foundation of the course. Education 1300 encourages students to apply various learning paradigms in order to make behavioral changes that will have a positive impact on their studies, as well as their role in society.

First-year experience courses can introduce students to Howard Gardner's theories of multiple intelligences, which can validate nine broadly defined intelligences and demonstrate how they are evident in a student's life. He or she may discover that his or her talent for drawing and an understanding of form and design might be an aspect of spatial intelligence. When examining Carl Jung's typology, a student may find out that his or her solitary nature, high sensitivity, and social cautiousness are typical of introverts. This insight might be useful when making decisions in the future.

The Myers-Briggs Type Indicator (MBTI) is an assessment tool that can help identify sixteen possible personality combinations. Students may discover a trait that in the past was viewed as a flaw, which might actually be connected to an integral part of their personality and can then be turned into an asset. Optimism, flexibility, and spontaneity may be part of an overall approach to life that, once understood, can help them make decisions differently.

Understanding emotional intelligence can assist in developing better self-awareness and lead to empathy and autonomy. Sometimes students discover that their emotions need to be managed better or tailored according to the environment of the college. All of these exercises can validate different aspects of a student's temperament and help him or her with critical thinking skills, reflection, and visualization, all essential in becoming a true lifelong learner.

VALIDATION THROUGH LEARNING COMMUNITIES

Another movement that has gathered momentum in higher education is the use of learning communities. Ironically, community college students often lack a sense of community. Typically, transient students leave campus, continue with their busy lives, and are seldom involved in the culture of college. Less engagement increases the risk of dropping out (Gonzalez 2009). Like first-year experience courses, learning communities appear to be particularly beneficial at community colleges, where large numbers of commuter students live and work off campus and are only on site during their scheduled class times (Minkler 2002).

Studies have now found that learning communities provide students extended exposure to peers, faculty, and staff and have the potential to build a sense of togetherness and cooperation, which typically does not develop in a more traditional college classroom setting (Minkler 2002; Shapiro and Levine 1999). Learning communities can create opportunities for these students to build networks, interact more closely with professionals and other educated people, and have access to the multiple benefits of campus life.

A learning community can create a feeling or a sense of closeness and intimacy, even when institutions are very large, thus leading to a greater coherence among students (Levine et al. 2004). Both learning communities and first-year experience courses provide substantial advantages and therefore, when paired, can have the potential to be an academic powerhouse that can "bridge the gap between what students bring to college and what they expect to take with them when they leave" (Levine et al. 2004, 9).

Retention rates and learning outcome results are usually improved and study and critical thinking skills are generally better enhanced in these paired courses (Levine et al. 2004; Swing 2002). In addition, these courses have the potential to promote learning that is more democratic and multicultural (Rendón 2000). They can increase students' intellectual confidence and foster social interaction among faculty and peers, while reducing students' self-consciousness (Smith 2010). The combination appears to be particularly useful for ESL students by bringing them into the mainstream college culture, while at the same time building on the knowledge that will help them in their transition and achieve success in a broader higher education setting.

At EPCC, a three-way learning community was developed to help a small cohort of Mexican American ESL students in their transition to academic transfer courses and into the college culture (Campa 2013b). The three-way learning community combined a first-year experience class (Education 1300) with ESL reading and writing courses to become an interdisciplinary combination, which created more "seamless learning environments" (Smith 2010, 262). The ESL students who enrolled in the learning community were typical of those studying at EPCC; many were from working-class homes and were struggling with a new language.

Students were encouraged to connect both inside and outside the classroom, between subjects, and among faculty and staff. In addition, the Education 1300 class included a few students who were not in the ESL program in order to encourage more diverse connections throughout the student body.

Each of the classes met separately but was shaped by shared goals and course themes. The faculty consulted regularly to develop a curriculum that validated students' experiences and learning and prepared them to transition into the broader culture of college.

The curriculum for this particular learning community was structured in ways that helped the students develop resilience. It included research projects, reflective papers, presentations of research findings, and discussions. By examining, studying, and learning about other individuals, groups, and societies that had experienced adverse circumstances, the participants were encouraged to reflect on their own worlds where similar struggles exist.

Making the Transition

Typically, ESL students are separated from traditional academic programs on campus, which leads to a curriculum that is not well integrated, placing students at the margins (Bollati 2006; Ignash 1995; Smith 2010). ESL students often feel insecure, lack confidence, and at times experience fear. Before these learning communities were developed, ESL students usually did not enroll in college credit courses until they completed the six-level program or took a placement exam. The learning community offered a new opportunity for students to take a credit course (Education 1300) while still being enrolled in the ESL program. It served as a bridge to the academic world and created validation.

Although ESL students were somewhat isolated from the general student body, many of them formed cohesive bonds and cultivated many friendships within their own community. Transitioning to college credit courses was a common topic of conversation among their peers who did not enroll in the learning community. They feared the change and were often uncomfortable with what they would encounter in academic transfer courses.

> Daniela: We all have that fear of entering into college classes. Everyone asked Abigail and me, "How is the class? How can you have five classes? Is it difficult?" So I would say, "You know what? You should try it! It's not that difficult because the three classes are related." You do have extra homework and extra assignments but we already know the topics. We know because we are learning similar things and topics. Those were some of the fears they had and that is why they did not enroll in the learning community.

> Interviewer: What do you think they are afraid of?

> Daniela: I think the transition. Even though we are adults we are afraid of something new. Not only is this new but we are also learning in another language. People are afraid of new things but as soon as they try it they realize it is not as terrifying as they were thinking.

The learning community certainly helped Daniela make the transition. This thirty-seven-year-old Mexican American married woman with two children is now a veteran of the process and is frequently sought out by her peers for advice. She has become an advocate for learning communities and is attempting to alleviate some of the trepidation experienced by her peers.

Language is a common obstacle among the participants and their Mexican American peers. In many parts of the world, speaking more than one language is seen as an asset, an opportunity for personal and professional growth. But for many of these ESL students, learning a new language is a hair-raising, anxiety-inducing experience that can be paralyzing at times. To make matters worse, ESL students are sometimes perceived as incompetent in academic areas because they lack English language skills (Pratt-Johnson 2006). Most of the participants believed that people who look and speak like them are "less than the intellectual norm" (Delpit 2002, 46). Their language skills are not seen as valid.

However, this did not become a self-fulfilling prophesy through validation. Instead the participants capitalized on their new beliefs and used them to cultivate their resilience. The students often spoke of having to work harder and put more effort into college projects and assignments because of their "deficiencies." Isabela, a twenty-one-year-old woman, learned to over-compensate for the "deficit" perspective.

> Isabela: *El curso es bien importante* [the course is very important]. I liked it [Education 1300] because we did so many activities. I also liked it because there were several of us ESL students in class. Other students spoke English since they were little and I liked that we interacted with them. I liked it a lot because we learned so much from them. And also we always have that pressure that we need to exert ourselves double the amount that they do. So talking and interacting with them really helped. I learned new things and new ideas.

Isabela is interacting and acquiring as much knowledge as possible from her native English–speaking peers. In addition, she found the learning community and the Education 1300 course particularly helpful as a validating experience for several reasons. Isabela laughed as she made a startling revelation:

> The projects required certain things and I noticed that many other students did not meet those requirements, but we did. That's when I thought, "We're not doing so bad!" We felt much better about ourselves. I also think that knowing that we had to over-prepare really helped us—thinking that they are more advanced and that we have to catch up to them. It was more pressure and it motivated us to work harder—*¡Dale, dale, dale* [go, go, go]*!*

Isabela is describing validation in action. Jalomo and Rendón (2004) report that "students who are validated begin to believe they can be successful; become excited about learning; feel a part of the learning community; become motivated; and feel cared about as a person, not just as a student" (43). In this particular situation, Isabela is being validated by the fact that she and her ESL peers are performing academically better in a research project than the non-ESL students in the same first-year experience class.

Because Isabela and many other ESL students perceived themselves as inadequate or "less than," this experience contradicted those beliefs and bolstered their self-confidence as successful college learners. During the individual presentations of their research findings, they all performed remarkably well and produced outstanding work. The presentations were organized, thorough, included excellent visual aids, and had strong social justice perspectives with detailed plans of action.

Overall, the quality was professional and much better than the presentations typically seen in an Education 1300 class. The professors were quite impressed with their performance. The ESL students explained that they had been working in their reading and writing learning community classes and were also meeting on their own time and practicing in the ESL labs. The students were "overcompensating," pushing themselves further and validating each other at the same time.

These improved outcomes were not an accident. The faculty, who taught in the learning community, met regularly to discuss the participants' performance and planned to integrate the curriculum in ways that "[found] the student's interests and buil[t] an academic program around them" (Delpit 2002, 45). Validation is not just about social connections and "being nice," but is instead about expanding on the brilliance of the students (Delpit 2006).

The faculty promoted integration, depth, and rigor in the learning community, where reading, writing, and research work overlapped. They also made sure that the participants had no choice but to learn. Although José María, a twenty-one-year-old man, was partly joking, he said it in the best way possible: "For example, when we read a book in one class we would discuss it in the other class, and then we would write about it in the third one. So you learn it because you learn it!" All of the participants spoke about the importance of conducting research in the learning community and its positive impact on their transition.

In addition, they found the topics of money management, time management, resilience, and social justice relevant and extremely helpful in bolstering their academic ability. Providing the participants with an environment in which they could learn to validate their own experiences was crucial to their success. It showed them that they were just as capable, and sometimes more productive, than their non-ESL counterparts.

Validating Gender Experiences

"Moving away from the everyday realities," or the world that they are familiar with, to "the new world of college" is a complex task for Mexican Americans and other minority students, especially those who come from a working-class background (Jalomo and Rendón 2004, 38). The lives of many students have been shaped by their cultural experiences, and the learning community was structured in ways that have helped them push back at these sociocultural forces within their home and society. Instead the students have ingeniously developed strategies to twist these fibers of adversity and transform them into a resilient yarn that has empowered them and their families.

The learning community helped validate the students' struggles, particularly among the married Mexican American female participants with children. These women told many stories about the challenges they faced every day in order to attend EPCC. The greatest problem they encountered in their transition to the world of college was pursuing their education while preserving traditional and gendered cultured norms. With frustration in her voice, Daniela disclosed the following:

> My husband is my number one obstacle. He is a *machista* and he told me, "As soon as you finish your English program, you are done!" That's what he told me because he believes, women should stay home—cooking, cleaning, and taking care of the kids. That made me angry! So I told him, "You know what? I need to do something else. When I am home I eat a lot. I'm getting diseases. I'm nervous. I need to do something! And it is not going to affect the family because my children are at school when I am at the college." As soon as I'm done with my classes I go home and cook dinner, help them with their homework, and everything is okay. But this attitude is my big obstacle right now.

As married Mexican American women with children, Daniela and the other participants have many responsibilities far beyond those of the typical college student. They do routine housework, prepare the family meals, help their children with their homework and extracurricular activities, and transport them to school, all while attending college, studying and writing assignments, and learning a second language. The lack of spousal support adds more strain to an overburdened life. This is the outcome of a Latino "peer culture that values women in the role of 'girlfriend,' 'wife,' and 'mother' to such an extent that there is a high social risk involved in displacing these roles with those of 'lawyer,' 'physician,' or 'professor'" (Gándara 1995, 92). In other words, the belief that women need to stay in their place.

Even Carmen, a thirty-eight-year-old mother of three children, who had more support from her husband than other women in her situation, was overwhelmed by these societal and cultural expectations:

> Because sometimes I think, "I need to go back to work. College is not for me. When I'm driving home from school, come down my street, and see my house that's when reality hits. I know my time is up." I try to put the house in order so I tell the kids do this and that! But then I think, "If I leave school then what?" I know I will still think that something is missing. I need to do something for myself because my kids will live their life. So even if I only take two classes, I will still feel like I am working on something for me.

At times the pressure to comply with so many traditional norms felt like a levee that was about to be breached. The female participants have often thought about dropping out of EPCC and getting jobs. They believed it would make things much easier. But instead they reflected on their dilemma and sought out the support of their peers. In the learning community, the participants generated creative strategies to deal with difficult circumstances.

Curriculum in the learning community included writing research papers related to careers and social issues while reading and discussing works of literature intertwined with themes of struggle, resilience, success, and social justice. Some of the selected works included *The Other Face of America: Chronicles of the Immigrants Shaping Our Future* by Jorge Ramos, *Night* by Elsie Wiesel, and *Mindset: The New Psychology of Success* by Carol Dweck. A learning community allowed the participants to construct a combination of simple and elaborate strategies, depending on their circumstances, to support their ambitions to withstand these forces.

Analyzing, synthesizing, and applying the concepts in Dweck's *Mindset* had such an impact on Daniela's life that she began to move beyond some of the culturally gendered obstacles. She attempted to steer male members of the family in different directions, something quite assertive for a typical Mexican American wife and mother. With validation, she became the teacher; she became the advocate and suggested readings for those in difficult circumstances, just as her professors had advised her.

> Right now I have an uncle who is in prison—here in the United States. So I told him, "I recommend that you read the book *Mindset*." He has a son and his son is having difficulty with gangs. I think my nephew is 14 and he told his dad that he did not want anything to do with him anymore. So I told my uncle, "Read this book because it will help you a lot. Because even though you are in jail, you are still his role model. You are still his father." He said, "You know what? I will read this book!"

Daniela's new passion for books and learning upset her husband. He viewed this as time taken away from the family. So Daniela artfully put her readings to work and made it part of the family's activities. For example, on Saturday mornings, when having breakfast with her son, daughter, and husband, the family usually discusses routine events that happened during the week. As a new strategy, Daniela began to interject lively, animated stories about the characters in some of her readings. She caught their attention, got them interested in the latest book she was reading, and afterward reported that "they are like, 'Wow! Really? And what happened next?'"

As a result, Daniela has become quite the storyteller and has brought a piece of her learning community and a fresh view of education and success into her home. What started out as a way to avoid conflict over her new role as an educated woman has now become a family tradition. Her husband has backed off and now begrudgingly enjoys some of the stories. Daniela has had her life experiences validated and is circumnavigating a course that will allow her to pursue her educational goals "without alienating [herself] from all forms of social and psychological support" (Gándara 1995, 92).

Like Daniela, Carmen also developed new strategies to challenge her family's ideas about gender and success. The Education 1300 class, along with the two other courses in the learning community, gave her a chance to reflect on her goals and aspirations. She found the first-year experience class to be extremely useful for goal setting and developing strategies. She soon began to turn it into a way to inspire and influence her son, integrating some of her family into the process and making it easier for the next generation to advance.

> I think the education class is a good class because it made me think. It's one hour that we usually use to think and see the best part of why we should study and continue with our classes. We think about our goals and of not giving up! When the class first started I thought, "I'm too old to get all that advice" but once I got into it I thought, "Wow this is a very important class!" All students should take that class. I was really excited and I told my son, "It's great, when you take that class, pay attention!"

Carmen brought her validation and motivation home, promoting education and success. Her son is now more excited about learning. She has also overcome various social pressures by persuading her husband to enroll in EPCC. Carmen skillfully took control of the family and changed their attitudes. Both her son and husband have become influenced by her studies. In essence, she has set a new direction for her family.

Through these and other experiences, the three-way learning community provided a means of validating the students. At first, Carmen and other female students in the learning community had all expressed some concern about confronting the traditional expectations of women in a Mexican American home. The learning community allowed them to experience these tensions together, connect to other types of struggle, and better understand some of the options they have had. By being validated, they have become more self-confident, motivated, and creative. Gender and machismo appear as common themes in their writing assignments and research projects as they continue in their community college course work, allowing them to see a larger purpose to their studies and their lives.

VALIDATION IN ACTION

Mr. Eliodoro "Lolo" Mercado is an academic counselor at EPCC and has been teaching Education 1300 since the course was created in 2001. His credentials are exemplary. He is a licensed professional counselor, a licensed counselor supervisor, and is certified and trained in countless specialties and practices. It takes a great deal of energy to regularly counsel students, stay up to date in a variety of fields, teach classes, and participate in a wide range of college activities.

To do so, this athletic, driven man rises early and runs a few miles each morning to warm up for a 7:00 a.m. class, followed by a full day of working closely with students. With a strong, fit physique, this fifty-something teacher resembles a young cross-country runner. But Lolo is proud of his recent gray hair because now the students see him "more as a mature person." This energetic, dynamic, friendly, and funny professor is highly recommended by EPCC students.

Julienne, a twenty-eight-year-old woman laughed and explained that "Lolo is my coffee at seven in the morning! He definitely wakes students up!" One of Mr. Mercado's true areas of expertise is validating students' life experiences and helping them find their "element," the intersection that Robinson describes where "natural aptitude meets personal passion" or "doing something for which you have a natural feel for" (2013, xi). When Professor Lolo Mercado is counseling or teaching, he is clearly in his element. He loves the activity and thrives on it.

But it took time to develop the passion and cultivate the skills. Lolo was born and raised on a farm near Friona, Texas, in the Panhandle area. His parents were hard-working immigrants from the mountainous state of Zacatecas who instilled the same ethic in their four children. As a young child, Lolo helped his family with the farm, and later worked in a tire shop to earn a few dollars so his parents could make ends meet.

By the time Lolo was in high school, the family had moved to Lubbock, where he enrolled in basic vocational classes. The decision seemed to make sense at the time, but his sister, a former valedictorian and a law student, ordered him to "go back to the counselor, immediately" and enroll in college preparatory classes, such as algebra and chemistry. He did and then entered Texas Tech University, where he was placed with a graduate student assistant who performed a career assessment on him. The student never really explained the results and simply gave him a list of careers to choose from. Without any guidance, Lolo just picked one, "Advertising sounds good enough!" He survived the program but clearly was not in his element. His artistic skills were limited and the few interviews he had led nowhere.

As noted before, family can be a powerful environmental protective factor. Once again, his sister intervened and suggested that he pursue a job with Talent Search, a university recruiting and counseling program. During the job interview he was asked, "Why should we hire you if you only have a degree in advertisement?" Lolo replied, "Because this job is about selling one thing—education—and I am very good at that!" Lolo was hired with the condition that he go back to school and earn credits in academic counseling.

While working on his master's degree in Counseling, Lolo experienced an energy that he never felt during his advertising studies. He became fascinated with skills, such as career planning, personality assessment, and family systems. "I was just like a sponge the whole time I was in graduate school." Before he finished his degree, Lolo was one of the first Hispanic faculty members to be hired at South Plains College in Levelland, Texas. There Lolo created the largest Mexican American student club in a predominantly white community and developed his career guidance skills.

In the early 1990s he accepted a counseling position at El Paso Community College. Lolo Mercado began to understand that something very basic was missing from many of the new students' experiences at the college. They lacked direction and had little knowledge of their own skills and abilities. He repeatedly saw one basic overriding problem: the students had no dream, no vision of their lives or careers, and had never had the opportunity to explore these ideas. Their life experiences had never been validated. They were certainly not in their element.

A few years later, when the Education 1300 course was developed, Lolo jumped at the chance to teach the class. "I think I was called to teach this class later in life because everything I teach the students I learned on my own—the 'hard way.'" Lolo's expertise and lifelong love for counseling and psychology is apparent in the classroom. Julienne shared the following:

> Lolo was my instructor and he made Education 1300 a really great experience. I took his course almost two years ago and still use a lot of the things he taught us in class. He gave us articles and taught us how to study for math and science classes. We also did a lot of listening activities in class and then we had to practice these in our everyday lives. He gave us a lot of inventories. I remember taking an inventory home and answering 300 questions about my likes and dislikes. Then we would find out if we should be a chef or a scientist.

Lolo has a thorough and holistic approach to career exploration. He helps the students to look inward, assess their strengths and weaknesses, and learn more about themselves. His students complete various types of inventories and work with him to understand the results. His background in career and psychological theories is phenomenal. He helps students learn about their personality types by asking them to complete psychological assessments, such as the MBTI or the Keirsey Temperament Sorter.

Lolo then uses his expertise to discuss the results of these assessments with each of the students. He narrates stories with many real-life examples to describe the various personality indicators. The students are then asked to role-play their opposite personality types. For example, students who are high on introversion are asked to act the part of an extraverted person. Eva, a thirty-year-old Hispanic woman and a former student, describes her experiences:

> We would work in groups and he would give us surveys. After we went over my results, I learned why I'm so talkative and bossy. I am a manager so I want things done a certain way. My thinking can be very black and white. So Mr. Mercado made me do the opposite and it was very stressful for me. And he said, "That's how the people that you deal with feel." And I used to always think, "Why are my employees so lazy?" And it's not so much that they are lazy but they have different personalities. So this helped me to learn how I was coming across and to understand other people.

Lolo also provides the class with scenarios and asks students to solve financial, relationship, and work-related problems. Then the students are asked to compare and contrast how their personalities influence their decision-making and problem-solving abilities. The students are asked to apply, analyze, and reflect this new knowledge so that they can understand more about their personalities and those of others. The students are also required to practice different activities with their families and friends in order to apply the theories learned in class in a real setting.

This is only the first of many steps. In addition, Lolo requires that students complete the Career Occupational Preference System (COPS) and other career assessments. Even though some of these concepts can be theoretical and complex, Lolo uses his expertise, experience, and personality to help students learn and apply these ideas. He is playful, authentic, uses his great sense of humor, and teaches con respeto. Eva explained that Lolo gave her and the rest of the students a degree plan outlining the course requirements for their career. The plan was based on what they learned about themselves.

Lolo then meets with his students outside of class as a counselor to provide them with further resources, advice, and mentoring. After Eva developed a keen interest in linguistics, Lolo sent her to consult an advisor at the University of Texas at El Paso. Because Eva is fluent in Spanish, Lolo recommended that she take a College Level Examination Program (CLEP), an exam at the university that would earn her twelve credit hours for speaking Spanish. Cristiano conveyed the following: "Even though I'm learning to help myself through the Education 1300 course, Mr. Mercado has helped me a lot. I play soccer and we've been looking at colleges where I can play soccer."

This resilient professor goes far above and beyond the call of duty to serve his students as a teacher, a counselor, and a mentor. Unlike Lolo's own college experience, his students walk out of his course with insight and knowledge about who they are, who they want to be, and how to get there. Lolo teaches in ways that are meaningful to students to validate their experiences.

Cristiano really liked Education 1300 because it was so different from his other classes. He explained that Mr. Mercado provided them with a lot of activities, undertook a hands-on approach to learning, and that in this class "the students talked and interacted with other students a lot more" than in his other classes. This is why, years later, students like Julienne and Eva are still applying what they learned in Professor Mercado's class. Eva reiterated that what she learned in the Education 1300 class helps her with a lot of the classes she is taking now. She added that "Mr. Mercado teaches you skills that you will use the rest of your life."

Classroom observations and student interviews confirmed that his expertise and resourcefulness are outstanding. His students commented that Lolo rarely taught from the textbook. Instead he uses his experiences and twenty years of training to bring the classroom to life. Eva explained the following:

> You could tell that Mr. Mercado knew all the topics really well because he made them really interesting. You can also tell that he likes what he teaches because he does it in a way that all the students can understand.

Lolo's resilience is strengthened by his sense of service. He uses his experiences and hard-earned wisdom to serve something greater than himself. As a licensed professional counselor, he is required to attend seminars, conferences, and workshops. Lolo integrates what he learns at these trainings directly into the classroom. He also supervises interns working on obtaining their licensed professional counselor (LPC) certification.

Even though his supervisory job comes with tremendous responsibility and liability, Lolo does not accept payment for his services. His gracious commitment to the field allowed the author to obtain her license years ago, a gift that will never be forgotten. His only condition is that his interns honor the counseling profession by giving back to the college, the students, and the community.

Lolo cultivates his larger sense of purpose through action and engagement in the community. He served as the president of the local Trans-Pecos Counseling Association and brings state-level counseling conferences to El Paso. Lolo is an active member of his church and is involved in volunteer work. He features the community in his classes by inviting guest speakers. On one occasion, he brought a professional from a local clinic to teach students about sex education and a coach to speak about exercise, weight management, and health. Students also tour the library in order to learn how to write research papers and create PowerPoint presentations.

His students said that what they like best about Lolo is "his attitude." Cristiano noted that "he is a believer in what he says." Lolo has a very down-to-earth attitude and tells it like it is. He has a sort of Governor Chris Christie of New Jersey "no-nonsense" approach to teaching and being. This aspect of his personality was cultivated by his upbringing. Lolo is in his element, where his greatest joy "meets the world's greatest need" (Greitens 2015, 119).

Lolo used to provide counseling services to inmates in the local prison system when it was allowed. He warns his students about the dangers of substance abuse. Lolo tells them, "I'm not Jesus, okay. I know how this stuff works." Even though it's still painful for Lolo, he tells the students the following:

> I had two brothers in prison . . . [but] I didn't visit my brothers in prison. I wrote to them but did not go to visit them. Why? When I needed them they were not there. They'd rather be out doing drugs.

When asked if his brothers are still in prison, Lolo said that they had since been released. His two brothers started their own construction business with Lolo's help. One of them now spends his free time back in the prison system, ministering to prisoners. Not surprising, Lolo always has stories like this one up his sleeve. Where do these narratives come from? Lolo's larger purpose is to serve others and he therefore spends a lot of his time helping students, professional interns, athletes, and people in the community and his church. He has very extensive contact with a great variety of people and is always learning something new. When trying to motivate his students, Lolo tells them the following:

> I see a lot of students that don't have the means. They don't have parents that provide for them. I see a lot of poor kids that come and they're hungry for food and knowledge. They tell you, "If I don't get educated I don't have an option here. There is nothing for me. My parents and my relatives are either in prison or are doing drugs. None of my family members have graduated from high school or have been to college. I want to be the one person that can make a difference."

Lolo remarks that he likes having these types of students in class. He urges his current students to be the catalysts who will "change everything for their entire family and for generations to come."

> If you can do it, then the rest of your loved ones are going to say, well, "Dale did it!" I can do it too! She had three kids, and raised them alone, and still got her degree. That role that you take on is going to be hell, but you can do it. You need to recognize that!

The students find Lolo's stories, knowledge, tools, and resources validating. Eva stated, "Mr. Mercado has shown us basically everything we need to succeed in college and in life." Lolo Mercado had once been a college student who faced many hardships and had to learn things "the hard way." He embodies what Navy Seal Eric Greitens describes in the following:

> Resilience is the virtue that enables people to move through hardship and become better. No one escapes pain, fear, and suffering. Yet from pain can come wisdom, from fear can come courage, from suffering can come strength—if we have the virtue of resilience. (2015, 3)

Lolo understands from his struggles that Mexican American college students require direct and hands-on assistance. Professor Mercado uses his expertise and experiences and teaches con respeto to give students the type of confidence now evident in Eva. In essence, he provides the students with an "enabling, confirming and supportive process" using in- and out-of-class agents to foster the academic and interpersonal development of his students. Lolo validates his students' experiences, helps them develop goals and visions, and weaves his own strengths and wisdom into their academic lives.

Chapter Five

Cultivating a Larger Purpose

When facing adversity, resilient people often discover they are part of something greater than themselves. What begins as a challenge can evolve into a personal mission and reveal a larger purpose to their actions and their life. Resilient students often find they are connected to and responsible for their families, their peers, and members of the community. These connections are revealed gradually, in layers, almost as a scaffold, and can determine not just a simple career choice, but also their greater role in the world itself.

Family and community play an important role in promoting resilience. Delpit (2006) argues that the link to families and communities, "or to something greater than our individual selves, can be the force that propels our [students] to be their best" (230). She believes that in college, many students are robbed of the opportunity to achieve greatness because the focus of their studies is usually based on a rather narrow goal: getting a good job. Personal enlightenment, growth, and greater purpose are seen as luxuries available to others, not something that can be obtained while preparing for the workforce.

Community college students sometimes enroll in classes to strictly pursue that basic goal, but through their studies they find that they can take on much larger tasks, such as changing their family's history, becoming an advocate, influencing their community, and changing the world.

FAMILY AND THE LARGER PURPOSE

Many of the students' parents could not directly help their children achieve their educational goals with money or academic advice, but they provided many other valuable forms of support. As he progressed, Angel began to see a larger purpose to his studies. He saw them as a way to challenge some of the Mexican American patterns and traditions that had caused problems in his family. Through education, Angel hopes to break the cycle of abandon-ment that is common in his family. His grandfather had abandoned his grand-mother and left her to raise ten children. His father left his mother as well, and she struggled to support the family.

His mother cared for his grandmother until she died and then later looked after her father, even though he had done little to help the family. For Angel, the fact that his mother continues to invest in his education emotionally, spiritually, and sometimes financially is her way of saying, "I believe in you," and he attributes his "respect for all women, family, and life" to the teachings of his sister, mother, and grandmother. On several occasions, An-gel stated that he truly admires women because they "strive throughout their lives to be accepted as equal by working hard outside and inside of their homes."

Angel is committed to the women in his life because they are the basis of his resilience. He has witnessed the struggles that they have endured and this has enabled him to move in and out of several worlds, worlds that he does not embody. Therefore the promise that Angel made to his mother of caring for her the way she had provided for her mother inspires him to excel in his classes at El Paso Community College.

Sometimes families contribute ideas and inspiration that allow students to begin to see their larger purpose. One form is the rich pedagogies of survival in family *consejos*, or sayings, that have a sort of folkloric knowledge and a base for traditional values. Consejos often provide a base for educational aspirations and motivational strategies. Delgado-Gaitan (1994) describes consejos as nurturing advice "that implies a cultural dimension of communi-cation sparked with emotional empathy and compassion, as well as familial expectation and inspiration" (300).

She believes that this concept is quite profound and is one that cannot really be conveyed through the English language. Consejos are subjective forms of knowledge, a form of education, which are often transmitted through oral tradition, passed down through generations. Consejos are pre-modern and span over long periods of time in traditional rural Mexican villages. An example of a consejo that is common among these families is the reminder to their children of the value of acquiring a formal education.

Parents and relatives frequently speak of the sacrifices they have made in order to secure a better future for their children. These families had few opportunities to attend school or receive any type of formal education. Now, living in a different country and a different time, they hope that their children can achieve something that they had only dreamed of. Amanda recalled one of the consejos imparted by her mother:

Dicén "Nosotros lo tuvimos así, pero ustedes tienén una oportunidad aquí. ¡Estudién! ¡Aprrovechén!" [They say, "It was hard for us but you have a lot more opportunities. Get educated! Take advantage!"]

Amanda's parents insisted that she put her heart and soul into school because they recognized that education was the vehicle to social and economic mobility. Her mother, Mrs. Martinez, had given birth to her at the young age of nineteen. Mrs. Martinez had been raised by a single mother, did not have a college education, and had to work most of her life in unskilled, low-paying jobs.

The following conversation shows how success was a pressing matter:

> Study, study, study! My mom would say, "You have to be somebody *para que no cualquiera te pueda humillar* [so that people cannot treat you in degrading ways]." *Mi mom me daba buenos consejos* about school [My mom would give me great consejos about school]. *Y por eso, yo siempre le hechaba ganas* [And that is why I would give it my best].

Mrs. Martinez, like many Mexican women from low-income, non-English-speaking backgrounds, recognized that her quality of life in the United States was significantly better than that of her relatives in Mexico, but she was also aware of the limited opportunities available to someone in her situation. Mrs. Martinez wants her daughter, Amanda, to be a *mujer luchista*, a woman who fights back in order to break through the barriers that can result from being a Mexican American woman from a working-class background.

Mrs. Martinez is passing along knowledge that is not typically understood in mainstream society, but plays an important role in supporting Amanda's resilience. Along the border, consejos provide almost altruistic inspiration and guidance. *El ejemplo es mejor que las ordenes* (Examples are better than orders or actions speak louder than words). *El conocimiento es plata entre los pobres, oro entre los nobles, y una joya entre los principes* (Knowledge is silver among the poor, gold among the noble, and a jewel among princes. Or knowledge is valuable to everyone). People are reminded that *El primero es el deber que el placer* (Duty comes before pleasure).

Amanda's mother has also given very specific advice. She has warned her daughter against getting married or having children before completing her bachelor's degree. Amanda worked diligently at EPCC first to make her parents proud and secondly as a moral obligation as the eldest child to serve as a role model for her two younger sisters and her brother. Amanda also thought it was crucial to relieve her parents, particularly her mother, of the burden of taking care of her.

> She was always very proud. I've always tried to take care of myself so that my
> mom doesn't have to take care of me. I don't want her to have to worry about
> my grades or that I have to study. I tell her that I will take care of myself so
> that she has time to take care of my brother and sisters so that they can do well.

Her success at EPCC was fueled by the commitment to socially uplift her family. What pushed Amanda to achieve greatness went far beyond "getting a good job."

The other participants have also begun to identify with something greater than themselves and see their work as a chance to change history. Angel believes that growing up without a father has motivated him to make his own marriage work and to do well in his studies at EPCC. He hopes to "break the chain or cycle" of inequitable treatment generated by his Mexican American, male, working-class background and change the future for his one-year-old son, Carlitos. Angel states, "I don't want to be my dad," referring to being raised in a low-income, single-parent home. Angel wants things to be very different for Carlitos:

> I take care of my son and I want to be there for him as much as I can. I want
> more for my son! I'm trying to respect him, even though he is a little boy and
> doesn't understand respect yet. This is still new to me. He is my first little boy
> and I think that he needs to see his father trying to help him so that he can help
> himself. When he grows up I hope he does the same and follows by example.

Angel has a deep desire to change the past, present, and future of his family. For him it is crucial that the hardships he and his family have experienced are not repeated. Rather than abandonment, Angel seeks to maintain cultural traditions of support that cultivate and create unity. A strong part of his motivation to learn is to share his lived experiences and pass on the knowledge to Carlitos.

He has developed a renewed interest in geology and a new curiosity about philosophy and government from taking classes at El Paso Community College. This has allowed him to raise Carlitos differently. He hopes this will help change the prevailing stereotypical image of Mexican American males as men who are uneducated, *macho*, abandon their families, and disrespect women. By empowering his son with knowledge early in his life and modeling a new kind of relationship with the women in his life, Angel hopes to change his future.

Another participant with a small child shares a similar history. Juan Pablo, a twenty-five-year-old student, wrote the following brutally honest, passionate essay. It is an essay that deeply touches many EPCC students and can spark extensive discussions in class:

When you think of someone's life being saved during a life-threatening situation, someone ordinarily thinks of a super hero/heroin, police officer, or a fire fighter saving the day. Well, I wasn't quite rescued by none of the above mentioned but by a baby boy born about three years ago. I wasn't saved from a fire or a natural disaster but from my own toxic and volatile lifestyle of drug abuse, selfishness, and career stagnation.

Before my son, Matthew, arrived in this world at the beginning of 2010, I was not living a very promising or fulfilling life. I was 18 years old at the time and had just graduated in 2008 from high school, so I was still kind of trying to figure out my place in the world. Having not found my "identity" during high school, you could say I was a bit of a late bloomer. I also wasn't very confident in myself, was often a pushover, and people often took advantage of me, whether it be financially or otherwise.

I did not attend El Paso Community College, EPCC, immediately after graduating from high school. Instead I was busy living a stagnant life working at a restaurant as a cook. I was working at a locally owned and operated restaurant that specialized in cooking fried chicken wings for minimum wage, at the time. The owner/store manager often smoked marijuana, snorted cocaine, and other various illegal drugs while on the job. He often harassed me into taking a break to smoke some pot at the back of the store. I also recreationally smoked with my "friends." To be honest, I never really liked smoking but was afraid I would not be able to find any other friends. I knew deep down I didn't want to but I just wanted a place to belong.

On top of the drug usage, I was a selfish and unappreciative individual in my adolescence. Never knowing or having a father figure in my life, my mother raised me by herself. She clothed me, put food on the table, and provided me with shelter. She worked full time as a bank teller and began attending college around the time I was entering puberty just as I was about to begin middle school.

Working a full-time job, going to school, on top of being a parent is not an easy feat. I suppose I was just upset from the lack of parental involvement in my life while I was growing up and acted out my feelings, but that's another essay all in itself. I began working at the age of 16 and seldom ever gave my mom any money to maintain the house. Although she wasn't there for me all the time, she was working very hard to build a better future for us. I just didn't understand at the time.

I failed to see the importance of having a higher education until I found out my girlfriend at the time became pregnant around the time I was 18, going on 19. Before that, I was satisfied with living a mediocre life as a restaurant cook or cashiering at Target later on after that. I was okay with using drugs on a daily basis. I was alive but wasn't awake.

The gravity of becoming a father then hit me like the force of two tons of bricks landing on top of me. I was both worried and scared of not being able to take care of this young innocent soul that was about to enter my world. I didn't want him to end up like me! I didn't want him to be ashamed of me! I wanted to be a great role model for this kid!

I immediately vowed to him while he was still in his mother's womb that I would be a father he could be proud of. A father he could look up to. I quickly set off to clean up my act. I stopped smoking pot immediately. I quit the

chicken wing restaurant cooking job and lost contact with my former employ-
er. I cut all ties with the delinquents I was associating myself with. My mother
and I became closer and have strengthened our relationship since through my
son. I enrolled myself at EPCC to pursue a college degree in nursing and
managed to get a job at Texas Tech University Health Sciences Center as a
Student Assistant. It doesn't pay as well as I would like but they are great with
my school schedule and they did open the door to get into medical school! I
was fortunate enough to stay out of jail. Thank God for that.

    My son, Matthew, saved me from myself. His arrival into this world had
such a deep and profound impact on my life for the better. Through him, I
cleaned up my act and now see my mother from a different perspective. I now
have a healthy relationship with her and am working hard to become a nurse.
If it wasn't for him, I wouldn't be where I am today. He saved me from falling
into an abyss and for that, I am incredibly grateful. I thank God every day for
sending me such a divine gift. He truly is my hero.

Both Angel and Juan Pablo have high hopes for their sons, Carlitos and Matthew, and are cultivating a larger purpose as they develop their own resilience. The idea that they are transforming the lives of their children by exemplifying what it means to be successful Mexican American students is an inspiration to them and many other students. As part of a new up-and-coming generation of Hispanic males, it is crucial to both Angel and Juan Pablo that their children witness and share their success. By graduating from a community college and moving on to a university, both fathers believe they will blaze a new pathway for their children and future generations of Hispanics.

COMMUNITY UPLIFT

These students lift their families as they climb and begin to play a role in uplifting their communities as well (Knight 2004; Villenas et al. 2006). They not only hope to model behaviors and values for their children, but also to impact the larger world around them. This desire for greater change has created a larger sense of purpose and has become an essential part of their worldview. Crista, who spent her childhood in the rural mountain village of Rio Bonito, Durango, senses her greater purpose:

    I already raised my girls. You have to always be making a difference in the
world. Having a purpose is important for my survival. Otherwise I get de-
pressed and don't want to get out of the bed in the mornings. That is why I try
to reach children.

Crista sees a bright future in children and takes pride in having helped to raise her younger siblings and then her daughters. As a result, she has developed a deep connection to children, something she believes is quite unique.

In her own academic struggles, she began to see an opportunity to teach as well as learn. Through teaching, she tries to help others, her newly found larger purpose. Crista had struggled to master the most basic skills. At the age of thirty, she finally learned to read, and it was an exhilarating experience. "Once I learned how to read, I could not stop reading. I never saw the world the same way again!"

Crista had discovered how transformational literacy was for her and soon developed a zealous commitment to teaching children how to read. She saw this as a mission, "I can communicate with children in a way that most people can't." She remembers how difficult it was for her and her family to survive and firmly believes that the next generation will need to be literate in order to "fend for themselves" in society. After a few semesters at EPCC, Crista realized that many of her Mexican American peers also had great difficulty with basic reading and math.

She combined her new reading and writing skills with those of her husband, Anthony, a math major, and together they created a tutoring team. They worked informally as volunteers and offered their services to those in need. Crista continued her efforts to help children, but recently the team has been meeting with fellow community college students. With no compensation, they have built a network at the college that helps many students in their studies. Tutoring children and community college students became a family affair that soon extended throughout the community. Crista continued to expand the network and encouraged her youngest daughter, Vanessa, to volunteer some of her time. Crista's resilience helped her use her power as a Mexican American woman from a working-class background to promote education and uplift a much broader Mexican American community.

As she started reading, Crista became more aware of politics, expanded her studies, and developed her skills as an activist. She has participated in forums, political debates, and activities outside the college, which provided many opportunities to build networks with people in her community. Attending these events, paired with her own experiences, has broadened her views of important social issues. She has participated in many efforts to bring about social change.

For instance, Crista became an advocate for the children and families who had fallen ill or had died of lead poisoning in a small settlement located near a smelter in her town. Crista wrote poetry that documented these families' stories and engaged in many efforts to stop the reactivation of a large copper smelter that had devastated many of her people. Her newfound exposure to analysis and theory helped her understand how she had been marginalized at times and how this oppression actually fostered her resilience (Collins 2000; Knight 2004; Kumashiro 2002). Crista continues to advocate for her people, serving as both a student and a teacher in her community. She is an activist who works in subtle and not so subtle ways for progress and social justice in her community.

Other participants have engaged in less visible, but equally effective, forms of activism, hoping to create individual and social transformation in their own families and communities (Delgado Bernal 2006). EPCC played a prominent role in providing Sofía with opportunities to act as an agent of change. She benefited tremendously from the college's Service Learning Program promoted by one of her professors, Mary Mooney, of the Sign Language Interpreter Program.

By majoring in sign language interpreting, Sofía had the chance to socialize and build rapport with the deaf community. During this process, Sofía met many interesting people, including Nancy, a woman who was of mixed descent, part Cherokee and part white. Mrs. Mooney explained that Nancy was a senior citizen who was deaf, in the process of going blind, alone, and in need of some company. When Sofía and a friend volunteered to help and visited her for the first time, they were very concerned by what they observed:

> We found her in conditions that . . . I told Gracie [a friend and classmate] there were some students that came last semester. How can you leave a person like that? You have to *no tener asco porque* [you have to not get grossed out because], I know there are a lot of people that do because she had cats. The cats didn't do it in the litter box so we had several issues. So I told Gracie, "We can't leave her like this! We have to keep coming."

What started out as a small service learning project for extra credit soon turned into a much larger purpose. For the rest of the semester, Sofía and Gracie regularly visited Nancy and tried to help her in any way they could. They went to a local center that aids the deaf to get her assistance, but when the nurses would knock on the door, Nancy refused to open it because she was afraid. So they asked other students in their classes to get involved. They all offered to help and took turns bringing Nancy food and cleaning her house.

Sofía spent many days talking to her new friend, especially on weekends and holidays. She found Nancy to be sweet, knowledgeable, and a great storyteller. When Sofía was leaving, Nancy would always ask, "Can you come back again?" Sofía would reply, "Yes, I'll be here Wednesday." Nancy would then say "Can you come Monday and then come back Wednesday?" The friendship grew but the next semester Nancy contracted the flu and then lapsed into pneumonia. Sofía describes what happened next:

> We visited her at the hospital and we kept her house clean. . . . I was there the day before she died and that was an experience that made me think, "I wonder how many people live like this? They are getting no help." That was an

experience that. . . . That is when I told Mary, "I think I want to work with senior citizens if there is an opportunity to work with them." It made me very humble.

Typically, activism is perceived as resistance that is made public and visible (Collins 2000). But Sofía engaged in a more private, subtle, and nontraditional form of activism. Sofía's sixth sense for survival made her keenly aware that Nancy's situation would require a collective effort (Delgado Bernal 1998). Nancy was truly marginalized because of her disabilities, age, low economic status, mixed heritage, and gender. When she realized that the established institutions were unable to fully do the job, she organized her classmates to help with the caretaking of Nancy.

Students filled in where social services could not and made Nancy comfortable and helped her access the basic care she desperately needed. Over time Nancy made many new friends. Working in the community with professionals and her classmates toward a common goal was a great lesson for Sofía. It made her service learning experience "an eye-opening one" that expanded her larger purpose. It made her conscious of the fact that there are many people like Nancy in her community. This engagement and experience became a motivating force in her decision to work with people like Nancy, and it clearly helped in strengthening her own resilience by helping her develop a larger purpose in life.

THE PUENTE PROJECT

Another avenue of resilience at El Paso Community College is the Puente Project, a national, award-winning, internationally recognized program that has been helping students cultivate a larger purpose for more than thirty years (Gándara 2004; Rendón 2002). Its mission is to increase the number of educationally disadvantaged students who enroll in four-year colleges and universities. It uses an interdisciplinary approach and emphasizes writing, counseling, and mentoring. Puente (the Bridge) provides students with a new pathway to success.

The Puente Project begins with the premise that the cultural experiences of Latino students count as a knowledge base and can be a valuable resource in motivating and preparing them to attend a university (Gándara 2004; Laden 1999). One goal is to emphasize that academic success is not solely an individual pursuit. It is about family, community, and purpose. Puente students are encouraged to "lift as they climb," raising the expectations and achievements of others along the way and becoming leaders in their own communities (Collins 2000; Delpit 2006; Knight 2004). Puente began as a university program but over the years, has expanded into high schools and community colleges.

Puente students are guided by faculty, counselors, and community mentors. Faculty can inspire students and move them through a tailored curriculum that can help them develop their larger sense of purpose. Counselors
play an important role in helping students define and pursue academic and
career goals. Community mentors, especially those who have graduated from
universities and have become successful leaders in their communities, serve
as role models and provide an additional level of professional and personal
support. Much of the academic work involves extensive collaboration with
peers, as students work collectively on assignments and projects.

Rigorous writing and intensive reading help students go beyond what
Delpit (2006) calls "catching up" and allow them to excel. Assignments
include critical essays, literary analysis, personal narrative, poetry, and com-
munity-based reports. This unique pedagogy and collaboration drive students
academically and also strengthen their identity and allow them to be empowered by their heritage and culture (Gándara 2004).

The program provides students with a curriculum rich in literature written
by Latinos, such as the novels of Sandra Cisneros, Sergio Troncoso's short
stories and essays, and the novels of Denise Chávez. For many it is their first
experience with this genre, and they are often surprised to find out that so
much literature has been written by and about Latinos. They begin to see that
they are part of something bigger, a world that they experience every day and
now will have a chance to study, analyze, and ultimately become a part of.
Instructors, mentors, and counselors share their own personal experiences
and struggles with the students, which often compliments the readings. Com-
munity-based folklore and research projects involve parents, family members, and neighbors.

When professor of English and Chicano Literature and coordinator for the
Puente Program Richard Yañez first encountered the Puente team and
learned about their broad characterization of *familia*, he found the concept
"amazing." By integrating familia into the college experience, "they sold me
on it." Richard stated that "familia is a tool. It is a strong force in my life. I
would not be where I am without the help of some family members."

> My mom is super intelligent but was not able to pursue her dreams because she
> was a woman who had two sons in her early 20s. My father was very laid back
> and bohemian and she had to provide for my brother and me. She took some
> classes later on but she struggled with structured classroom settings. I think for
> different reasons. She did not have support systems the way I did. It was a
> different time. My wish would be that one day she would get a degree so that
> she could walk across the stage.

Professor Yañez candidly shares this and other stories with his students.
Often parents think of their children as extensions or mirrors of themselves
and try to project their desires upon them. Sometimes parents advise their

children to major in careers that will yield external rewards, such as wealth and status. Richard's mom wanted her son to become a lawyer and enjoy those external rewards rather than pursue the life of a writer. But Richard chose to work toward something larger, focusing his efforts on careers with internal benefits. He searched for a place to grow and expand his natural talents, to be in his element.

Success becomes complete when talents are shared with others, as Richard Yañez does through his writings and in his classes. He appreciates the sacrifices his mother made that allowed him to ultimately pursue his dreams. This taught him the importance of familia and how the students' cultural knowledge contributes to their educational success. Because "we teach who we are," Richard's experiences and ideas of familia have a powerful influence on his college teaching.

Richard is mindful of mentoring his students. He noted, "We are the frontlines of learning and that is a challenge. But I also see that we have to show them models of success in different ways. The students really respond to that." He holds regular one-on-one conferences with his students and encourages them to be a resource for each other. He makes use of technology and social media to create a network of support and encouragement. Students text their peers, remind them of upcoming deadlines, check up on absent colleagues, and motivate those who are falling behind. Students also meet and present to each other on topics such as planning, goal setting, and time management in an effort to build familia.

Richard calls his students *Puentistas*. One student, David, has already sensed a larger purpose to his work. He sees himself mentoring future Puentistas after he completes his studies at El Paso Community College and earns his degree. He hopes to explain how much this program has guided him through his academic career and changed his life. Richard Yañez's class lives by the motto "Once a Puentista, always a Puentista."

Richard is well connected in the writing community and has invited many of his literary friends to Puente. For example, his students had a chance to work with Sergio Troncoso, who grew up in nearby Ysleta, graduated from both Harvard and Yale, and has become a world-renowned author known for his short stories, essays, and novels. Many have a strong Chicano focus, emphasizing the role of heritage and culture in the borderlands. Four Puente students interviewed Troncoso, discussing his experiences growing up in the Lower El Paso Valley and his many accomplishments. The class then reviewed the video and edited the work so that it could be uploaded on YouTube.

Richard, like the other professors highlighted by the students, often uses teaching strategies that help his students learn in ways that validate their heritage. He creates curriculum that allows participants to bring their personal and intellectual experiences to class. During one class visit, Richard began the session by asking students if they were aware of any important events that had taken place over the weekend. One student mentioned the demolition of the American Smelting and Refining Company (ASARCO) smokestacks, the last remaining structures at the former smelter complex.

ASARCO evokes very deep personal feelings in El Paso. As the main metals smelter of the American Southwest, ASARCO had been an important part of the local economy for more than one hundred years. It had provided many generations of El Pasoans with good paying jobs and benefits.

But there was a dark side to the ASARCO story. For decades, the complex had contaminated the region with deadly toxins, especially lead, and had caused extensive health problems and damage to property. Smeltertown, a small community of mostly Hispanic workers and their families, was particularly affected. Lead poisoning had destroyed the health of many residents, especially children, who were constantly exposed to those particles in the air and soil. The contaminants were so predominant that the entire community had to be evacuated, condemned, and razed during the 1970s.

In the 1980s, the smelter complex received a thorough overhaul and, with new environmental laws and regulations, became a model employer once again, providing thousands of area residents their livelihood. The smelting business declined in the late 1990s, and by the early twenty-first century, the large ASARCO smokestacks, looming over Interstate 10 and visible throughout the city, were the last remnants of the complex. The decision to demolish the stacks divided the community. Some had hoped that demolition would finally close the book on a tragic chapter in the city's history.

Others had hoped that the smelter would reopen and be a major employer once again. Still others saw the stacks as something symbolic, a landmark to be preserved and protected. Other locals shed tears. One of Richard's friends, who lived in the Calavera neighborhood near ASARCO, couldn't stop crying as she expressed, "There is a lot of history there." ASARCO represented opportunity and community to some. During the late twentieth century, the smelter offered good jobs and built a strong sense of community among the small surrounding neighborhoods like Calavera. After watching a video clip of the demolition of the stacks on YouTube, some of the students felt grief while others celebrated.

Richard then had the class read a poem, "Ode to Adobe" by Pat Mora. He explained that an ode is a way of "exalting something." It pays tribute to or celebrates an idea or an object. Mora pays tribute to adobe, capturing its appearance, aura, and cultural significance. The students read Mora's poem and discussed the greater cultural meaning of adobe. This led to a larger discussion of landmarks and symbols, such as the stacks. Students discussed other local landmarks, what they represented, and what emotions and images they evoked.

Richard shared one of his works, "Ode to Chico's Tacos." Chico's is a popular local fast-food restaurant frequented by many of the students. The ode created an image similar to that of Mora's adobe. It captured sights, aromas, and the memories of Chico's recalled by Richard as a young boy. The classroom experience was almost magical, leading students to remember and imagine as they began to write about their favorite landmarks. Eventually, as their odes were created, they presented them to other students at a poetry reading at *Papagayo*, the college's writing club.

Professor Yañez provoked his students to think critically. During class, he asked the students many questions, such as "Why should Latinos write their own stories?" Santiago, a nineteen-year-old Mexican American student, responded, "to celebrate our culture, family, community, and life." Richard followed up with another question, "Are there things about our culture that we don't want to celebrate?" Another male student responded, "I don't want to have to work as hard as my father. His job is hard and a lot of times he gets frustrated. I am going to stay in school so that I can have a different job." Richard encouraged authentic conversations about the complexities and realities of culture.

Outside the classroom, Richard spent countless hours mentoring the Puentistas. Dante, a nineteen-year-old student, tells the story of how he lost his mother while he was a freshman in high school. She died of complications due to arthritis at the young age of forty-three. Richard Yañez helped him through a difficult time in his life.

> My mother passing away during my freshmen year really had a big impact, but I still managed. I went to school the next day after she passed away. A lot of my friends were like, "What are you doing here?" I'm like, "Well, I mean life keeps moving on and I can't just keep this image of my mother inside of me— just haunting me." I decided to do this because bad things happen and it's part of life. I need to keep moving forward especially the first year in high school. I wasn't going to let it destroy me or break me emotionally to the point where I just gave up on school.

Dante joined Puente and was placed in an Education 1300 student success course paired with a basic English composition class. He was particularly indebted to Mr. Yañez, his English professor, for playing an important role in his "wonderful first year of college." Dante was still recovering from the loss of his mother and the impact it had on his family. Like many college students, he lacked direction, structure, and had trouble adjusting to the many changes experienced as a freshman. Mr. Yañez always extended himself to the students and was generous with his time. Dante was lost, lacked direction, had too much freedom, and was falling behind in some of his classes. However, he took advantage of the information he was learning in Puente. He felt comfortable asking Mr. Yañez for help.

When you go into his office he welcomes you with open arms. All you have to
do is take advantage of the fact that he is willing to help you and all you have
to do is to ask him what you need.

Professor Yañez had met Dante's father during Puente's *Noche de Familia* (Family Night) and was aware of the struggles the family had been
through. Dante had a great deal of admiration for Professor Yañez, a teacher,
mentor, and Chicano writer. He liked the "type of person Professor Yañez is
and the way he carries himself." He stated, "I get a very good vibe even just
walking into the classroom." At times, Dante still hears his professor's voice
emphasizing the importance of reading in order to expand his vocabulary.
Professor Yañez would stress, "Read, read, read because that is how you
learn!" Dante developed qualities that helped him become a great mentee,
which are integral to a mentoring relationship.

He appreciated the fact that Professor Yañez exposed his college students
to many authors who wrote about El Paso and the border region. Dante was
excited that someone was writing about the city he lived in. After reading
Professor Yañez's book, he thought, "Wow, I have lived in and visited a lot
of the places that he is describing! I feel proud being from El Paso because
someone is actually writing about my city." Dante saw himself as part of the
course curriculum, part of a world larger than he had ever imagined, and
began to think about his greater purpose.

Richard's experiences from his childhood and adolescent years helped
him understand students like Dante and also provided him with a lot of
material to write about. Because his father was not particularly supportive,
Richard's mom had to work long hours. Richard's father was an only child
and was very poor when he was growing up. His father's parents helped raise
Richard and his brother. He was unable to go to a daycare or attend a pre-
school and therefore spent a lot of time with his grandmother, Chuy, and
grandfather, Apolonio. He believes that his grandparents "molded" him "in
every sense of the word" and that even though he "had so much education,"
their teachings were a blessing and served as a foundation for his future
growth and development. He adds, "I learned how to be a writer before I was
five." He fondly remembers his *cuartito*, a small room alongside his home
where he practiced writing as a child and envisioned himself someday becoming an author.

Richard teaches his students about symbols. Richard attributes his cultural and religious values to the influence of his grandmother and believes that
La Virgen de Guadalupe (the Virgin of Guadalupe), patron saint of Mexico
and Chicano icon, is an important cultural symbol that keeps him connected
with his grandmother. Even though it has been twenty years since grandmother Chuy passed away, Richard remembers her well and wrote a story

about her in this first book. Richard often says, "I have her chin. I love my grandmother, and I embody her."

All of Richard's grandparents were from small, humble towns in Mexico. His maternal grandfather came to the United States to work even though he was only eight years old at the time. He shined shoes as a young boy and eventually worked his way up and opened a dry cleaning family business in El Paso. His grandfather "had an amazing work ethic." He seized the opportunities on this side of the border and even named his business American Dry Cleaners.

Richard grew up in Ysleta in El Paso's Lower Valley. After he graduated from college with a master's of Fine Arts in Fiction Writing, Richard taught in the English Department of Colorado College as the Riley Scholar-in-Residence. Before joining El Paso Community College, he taught at Saint Mary's College in Indiana and wrote *El Paso del Norte: Stories on the Border*. In 2011, his second book, *Cross over Water: A Novel*, was published. Richard's writing and teaching are a celebration and a tribute to his community.

In these ways, the faculty at El Paso Community College helps students cultivate a larger purpose for their studies and in their lives. Changing the histories of their families, working for disadvantaged members of their communities, lifting them as they climb, inspiring them to be mentors, and creating a greater awareness of their culture adds greatly to their resilience and helps the students follow a new pathway through the community college, on to the universities, and out into the world.

Chapter Six

Building Social and Cultural Capital

Once resilient students have been validated, have discovered a larger purpose, and are on the pathway to a successful college career, they can begin to make use of the social and cultural "capital" that they have accumulated and invested in along the way. Stanton-Salazar (2004) describes such capital as "connections to individuals and networks that can provide access to resources and forms of support that facilitate the accomplishment of goals" (18).

Students coming from traditional middle- or upper-class backgrounds usually bring a certain amount of social capital with them when they enter college. They may have college-educated parents, advanced skills preparation, family and social relations with professionals, or experiences that have linked them to the broader academic world. Family members can guide them through the process and can often relate to their own college experiences. Community college students, especially the nontraditional minority students described here, are less likely to have this capital in reserve or be able to understand how it can be acquired or developed.

Social capital operates like monetary capital and can be saved, invested, exchanged, or withdrawn. It can be converted into forms of power, wealth, authority, and social influence and is therefore vital for cultivating resilience. Once accumulated, it can compound and turn into a powerful reserve. As the resilient student builds social capital and succeeds in life, he or she can function like a philanthropist and distribute his or her surpluses to others in need.

Social capital is the pathway to cultural capital, educational and intellectual knowledge, qualifications, skills, and abilities that will help a person achieve success in society. Once a student has cultivated these connections and becomes comfortable in the new educational or professional world, he or she can make use of his or her cultural capital to be admitted to academic programs, access scholarships, befriend faculty and professionals, and function in mainstream society.

A student can acquire social capital in a number of ways. It may be as simple as developing a friendship, taking part in a group project, joining a club or association, or by entering the nurturing environment of a classroom where he or she is taught con respeto. However, more formal relationships can generate greater social capital and lead a student to the cultural capital needed to proceed in his or her studies. Social and cultural capital will eventually allow the student to achieve larger, long-term goals, such as entrance to a competitive program, a fulfilling professional job, further academic studies, and eventually a more holistic, satisfying, content life. It can be the final step to happiness.

Some of the ways that El Paso Community College students have acquired and developed social capital are by "playing the game," weaving social webs, participating in learning communities, and entering into relationships with mentors. After accumulating some degree of social capital, the resilient student can confront his or her discomforts and fears and present him- or herself to the world.

"PLAYING THE GAME"

Some students began to understand early on that establishing connections and building relationships were becoming vital to their success. They dabbled or experimented with the process, developing techniques that allowed them to "play the game" and build capital. They invested in this process with a certain artfulness and discussed strategies that they had learned along the way in their educational journey.

Amanda described this artfulness as an understanding of power and how to maneuver within it, which is often difficult for minorities, and especially for women. Amanda learned that other students' accomplishments and achievements at El Paso Community College, as well as their new successes in life, were partly due to this resourcefulness. She noted that "we all here know how to play the game. We know how to do it. We are survivors! We really are!"

This refers to surviving in "the culture of power" (Delpit 1995, 24). Delpit writes that there are rules or "codes" for participating in power, rules created by those who have the power. The students refer to this as "playing the game" because, much like the culture of power, games are composed of rules. They explained that these rules varied from one setting to the next and that certain cultures often shared similar rules.

The codes were frequently evident in classrooms at El Paso Community College. One set of codes involved engaging in overt behaviors, behaviors that students are often uncomfortable with. These can help make a good impression, create a connection, and lead to social capital. A second set of codes involved building stronger links with their professors in order to go beyond social capital to access cultural capital (Gándara 2002).

Several resilient students were surprised at how little their fellow college classmates understood the social skills and behaviors needed to play the game. Robert explained that

> there is a *dicho* [saying] that says, *"Se agarrán más abejas con miel, que con sal"* [You can catch more bees with honey than with vinegar]. Like in my classes, I see some of the students that are younger than me. . . . I'm 32. . . . They treat the professors really bad. They don't have a boundary and respect. . . . They ask me, "Why is it that you get along well with your professors?" I tell them. *Es que les tienes que seguir la corriente* [You have to go along with their flow]. That's "playing the game!" You have to participate. Don't just sit there acting all bored. What really gets me is that they are texting [with their cell phones]. It gets me mad. I can't even imagine what it does to the professors.

Robert's dicho, "You can catch more bees with honey than with vinegar," comes from his strong family tradition of *buena educación*, or good upbringing, which taught him that kindness and respeto are crucial to success (Villenas and Foley 2002). Then he makes a concerted effort to explain to his junior classmates that in order for them to do well in their courses, they have to *"seguir la corriente,"* or "play the game." Robert takes it one step further by emphasizing one particular rule to abide by in college that his peers do not seem to understand: that of actively participating in class.

He explains that participating included engaging in class discussions, conversing with the professors, and attending extracurricular activities. He points out that behaviors such as texting in class, arriving late, or appearing bored and disconnected can create a deep impression in the teacher's mind that has negative consequences. Hence their opportunities to acquire social capital will be limited. A professor may overlook students who appear disconnected and concentrate instead on the others who understand these rules better and have developed new behaviors, consciously or unconsciously.

Robert is proud of the fact that he has attended classes every day:

> Actions speak louder than words. For example, the whole entire semester, I have not missed a class . . . the professors see that. They know who is there and who comes in late. They know who read the material and who is just slacking off. These are unspoken rules. They are actions that they observe. Be prepared. . . . Don't have your iPod on!

Robert has clearly learned that in the game of academia, reading the assignments and attending classes are some of the "unspoken rules" that often define what it means to be a "good student." Some of these behaviors are related to culture. Unlike the typical white middle-class student who is comfortable with these codes as a part of their culture, Mexican Americans, once they leave the classroom, can recognize that the game is over and return to their world, where they can maintain their cultural integrity when they interact with other Hispanics.

WEAVING SOCIAL WEBS

The expansion of social competency into webs or networks can lead to the acquisition of cultural capital. Mexican American community college students, especially those from lower socioeconomic status, may not understand the rules, but they probably have a basic social foundation to build upon when they first enter college (Gandara 2002; Stanton-Salazar 2004).

When students were asked what characteristics their family and friends liked most about them, they often responded with descriptors such as charming, enthusiastic, sociable, and good communicators. For example, Angel said, "My mom likes that I am very charismatic with people. I have the same strengths that she has because my mom can be really great with people." In other words, they had already learned some of these skills at home or at school, as well as other important protective factors, and are now learning how to apply them in college. Many times these overlapped and led them to more complex relations among students and peers. Angel built a social web that eventually included students, faculty, tutors, and people in the community.

Crista built on her social skills as she became a more successful student. The social networks that she wove with her peers, college personnel, and faculty provided her with the basic social capital necessary for her development and led to the attainment of cultural capital. She participated more broadly in college and community events and achieved a comfortable level of interaction with a variety of very different people. In an interview, she describes some of the benefits of social competency:

Crista: We have developed here [at EPCC]. There was a lot of development that we were lacking when we first came here, at least in my case.

Interviewer: What helped you to develop?

Crista: Just the opportunity to be here [at EPCC] and meet the people who offer the help and the services to get you through those times. . . . All that support that you get from your professors.

In her case, the challenges she encountered were a bit more extreme. As an older Hispanic female from a rural Mexican village who learned to read at the age of thirty, she felt that she was just as alienated from the student body as she was from the faculty and staff. Moving out into the community was even more frightening. Building social relations with her teachers and being validated in her classes helped ease the transition and led to a considerable degree of social competency.

Eventually, her teachers knew her well and provided the support she needed. For example, at one point in her studies, she became anemic but did not realize how ill she really was. During an important exam, Crista felt odd, a bit disoriented, as if her "brain was scrambled." Even the simple directions on the test did not make sense. Fortunately, she had already established a good relationship with her professor and was comfortable enough to explain what was happening. She notes that early on in her student days, she might have just tried to hurry up, finish the work, and accept the consequences. But in her professor's eyes, she had already "proven herself as a hard worker." He was more concerned about her immediate condition and later gave her an opportunity to take the test again.

Robert also understood the importance of social skills and behavior when dealing with his teachers:

> It's all about networking. I like to build a certain relationship with a professor because what if I apply for a scholarship and I need a letter of recommendation. "You know what, Mr. Joe Old; I'm applying for such and such scholarship can you write something about me?" Or if I need a letter from a professor stating what kind of student I am. Then when they are writing it they will remember, "Hey this guy participated . . . he asked questions, he was motivated." They are going to have a lot of stuff to write.

Robert clearly understood that professors, because of their status in academia and in society, could help him enter middle-class culture. For Robert to climb over his working-class status into middle-class society, it was going to require much more than professors knowing his name. That letter might serve as a pathway into a competitive program or it might connect him with a new circle of colleagues. Making this a reality meant taking those social ties and expanding them, turning them into cultural capital. Stanton-Salazar (2001) describes access to the middle class as a "social freeway" that can lead to institutional resources, career collateral, political connections, and many other advantages (17).

Mentoring

Mentoring is one of the most common ways to acquire social and cultural capital. In her best-selling book *Lean In: Women, Work, and the Will to*

Lead, Sheryl Sandberg, the chief operating officer at Facebook and former vice president of Google, describes mentoring as a strong relationship that is born out of "a real, and often, earned connection felt by both sides" (2013, 67). Sandberg found that mentoring was especially important for women who were often discouraged from being leaders or passed over for tasks that required a considerable amount of responsibility or for promotions.

Mentoring helps build resilience through caring interactions that convey high expectations. In solid mentoring relationships, people work harder and do more for the people they love and trust (Benard 2004). It is a mutual relationship that benefits both the mentor and the mentee. It is much more than just "meeting the right teacher; the teacher must meet the right student" (Palmer 1998, 21). Students cannot simply be paired with a mentor. "Intuitively, people invest in those 'who stand out' for their talent or who can really benefit from help" (Sandberg 2013, 68). Students need to ask themselves "What was it about [me] that allowed great mentoring to happen?" (Palmer 1998, 21).

Brooklyn grew up in a restricted environment and developed a very different view of the world through her studies at El Paso Community College. She shared that it was my class that piqued her interest in psychology. As Parker J. Palmer wrote, "The power in our mentors is not necessarily in the models of good teaching they gave us . . . but in their capacity to awaken a truth within us, a truth we can reclaim years later by recalling their impact on our lives" (1998, 21). Knowing that I awakened a truth within her that will impact her future validates my work as an educator and strengthens my sense of purpose.

Over time I developed a close mentoring relationship with Brooklyn. I guided her through her studies, helped her make the transition to the University of Texas at El Paso, and met with her regularly as we discussed graduate school opportunities in psychology. Brooklyn had become a focused, resilient student and built social capital through our relationship. I gladly helped her with whatever I could.

As "we" applied to graduate programs around the country, Brooklyn learned how to leverage cultural capital and apply her knowledge, skills, and resilience to the application process and the interviews. I was excited to write that

> I selected Brooklyn to participate in a study of resilient Hispanic community college students. She has faced and overcome many obstacles. Brooklyn is one of the most resilient students I know and we continue to have a mentoring relationship. During our visits, we discuss psychology, research, careers, and other topics. She is currently a member of the Tau Sigma National Honor Society and recently graduated with honors from the University of Texas at El Paso. Brooklyn's achievements exemplify resilience.

The letter placed Brooklyn in a unique position. She was an academically strong student and had the skills and abilities necessary to become a psychologist. She was interested in a research field and my letter went on to say that she had already participated in an important study of resilient Hispanic students, allowing her to experience some of the work that she would encounter in graduate studies. Distinguished and already a part of the scholarly world, Brooklyn was making use of cultural capital, showing that she would fit nicely in the various social science departments we considered.

This gave her an edge over hundreds of other candidates and eventually gained her and fourteen other applicants entrance into a distinguished institution, the University of San Diego, in a highly sought-after program. I thoroughly enjoyed working with Brooklyn and was as excited as she was when she packed up and headed off to California. Brooklyn had been validated, had built resilience, and through social and cultural capital was able to achieve a much larger goal.

Amanda also used her newly acquired capital to transition to university studies and enter a profession. We worked together on an application and essay that earned her the prestigious El Paso Community College Presidential Scholarship to help her with her studies. The family consejos (folk sayings) certainly paid off as she worked her way through EPCC and transferred to New Mexico State University. By then Amanda had developed interests in education, psychology, and counseling and pursued coursework in those fields.

She continued to build her social capital, participated in several research projects, and kept in contact with me throughout. Amanda acquired additional cultural capital by establishing new relationships at the university. She graduated, passed her certifications, and landed a teaching job in the Ysleta Independent School District on the east side of El Paso. In addition, Amanda has already begun investing her social capital. For more than six years, she has been a mentor for El Paso's Big Brother-Big Sister Program. In the meantime, her cultural capital has expanded even further. She became acquainted with and married into a family of counselors. She continued teaching for the district and recently entered a graduate program in counseling at the University of Texas at El Paso.

BALANCING RESPETO AND AMBITION

Higher education is essentially competitive and, for better or worse, it focuses on the development of the individual. Although there has been a lot more emphasis on groups, cooperative projects, and communities in recent decades, the typical college student needs to perform well, distinguish him- or herself from others, and set his or her own trajectory in order to succeed.

Culture can sometimes interfere with the development of basic social capital by placing less emphasis on the individual.

Some El Paso Community College Mexican American students described how their cultural background was riddled with contradictions that often made it difficult to make the transition into mainstream college culture. Understanding and confronting contradictions was a serious challenge, but one that greatly added to their resilience. Mexican American families often affirmed and reinforced the tradition of buena educacíon with an emphasis on humility, respeto, and collectivism (Villenas and Foley 2002).

At home they learned respeto as a form of respect, but also one of deference. Challenging elders or veering away from social norms was viewed as impolite, even threatening at times. Asking questions, seeking attention, and distinguishing themselves as individuals was often seen as indicating *"falta de respeto"* or a lack of respect. Because the main goal of many of these families is to succeed as a unit, the individual children were not the primary focus. Instead they were often prompted to contribute to the collective goal by "function[ing] well within the system as a whole, neither disrupting its balance nor causing the family to devote its energy to nonessential concerns" (Valdés 1996, 117). Children were discouraged from being the center of attention.

This creates problems when Mexican American students enter mainstream culture and have to balance conflicting sets of values and behaviors. Sofía sensed great tension and attributes her poor academic performance in her early years to the clash between the *sabiduría*, or traditional knowledge, instilled in her by her family and the values, beliefs, and behaviors of the school setting:

> I remember going to school, and it was usually the white boy or white girl in the class who had the highest grade. He was the good little boy, the teacher's pet. You wouldn't see a *Mexicano* doing that. I guess I was taught that I should not bring attention to myself. I was taught to be quiet and *humilde* [humble], don't attract attention, don't speak too loud!

Sofía was receiving mixed messages from two different cultures. At home her buena educacíon was revered and at school it was refuted. Buena educacíon does not fit well in the competitive culture of American public schooling. The behaviors that were encouraged, to compete and earn good grades, were unacceptable at home, leading her to say that you "wouldn't see a Mexicano [Mexican person] doing that."

Crista observed some of the same tensions. She saw a sharp distinction between the beliefs of her Mexican American peers and those of a white middle-class family:

> In the white culture, children are taught to speak up, ask questions, and that it is okay to interrupt. They are encouraged to say blessings and they are validated for doing these things. In our homes only grandma or grandpa can do these things. It is considered disrespectful to speak up and ask questions. I know. I got into a lot of trouble for doing this.

Her actions were seen as offensive, as going against the teachings of her family, and as a female, even more of a threat. Male students also spoke about the importance of respeto and humility.

Robert explains that when growing up he too was taught not to ask inappropriate questions. But the females faced the stronger traditional values associated with being a *Mexicana*, a Mexican woman. Sofía noted that her "parents are from the *rancho* [a rural upbringing] and the women are *bien sumisas* [very submissive]. Whatever the man says is what goes." Not only are there gender differences in how these children are raised, but there are also variations among socioeconomic classes. In the lower socioeconomic classes, a buena educacíon is more prevalent and usually more extreme. In the upper socioeconomic classes, the basic principles are still there, but they are more diffuse and less rigid at times.

The behavior of the white middle-class children observed by Sofía and Crista would probably have been seen as disrespectful by their families, but it taught these women important lessons in resilience. They began to understand that these behaviors were needed to truly succeed. After Sofía saw how these children were rewarded, she confessed that she "wanted to be a white girl." Later Sofía realized that she did not really "want to be" or want to take on the identity of a white girl. Instead she wanted to enjoy some of the success, while maintaining a balance with her cultural values.

She discovered that she was more comfortable in between the two polarities by showing respeto and being a bit more assertive. Sofía and the students learned early on that they can preserve their buena educacíon and at the same time can function in mainstream society without "acting white" or fully embracing the middle-class values (Fordham and Ogbu 1986). Robert agreed and said that in order to achieve academic success at EPCC, "you have to know when to be Mexican, when to be American, and when to be both."

Crista went further and took on more of an assertive role:

> You need to be more outspoken. You need to say, "Excuse me you opened up a can of worms, now support it!" I don't have a problem even asking my professors that question especially if they open the question. I will ask them to answer my question. I'm nice about asking. That really helps me to speak without being shy. I have been in that place that you are talking about where you take eight steps forward and ten steps backward because in our culture we are taught to be shy.

For Crista, going back and forth between what she considers being Mexican and being American is an ongoing struggle. Yet she finds a middle ground where she is able to be both. Crista shows her respeto by listening attentively and critically. Then she politely asks the professors and other students to support their arguments. She said, "you need to let go of being shy. That used to be my problem. You need to let go of that shyness and be more assertive. That has really helped me a lot. I was always scared to ask." Balancing respeto with the ambitions and aspirations of being a student was a delicate process, but one that was necessary to move through their college studies and out into the world.

LEARNING COMMUNITIES

Learning communities parallel credit classes with the same students and make use of several faculty members who work together to create a common curriculum. These classes can create a strong sense of togetherness and help participants work collaboratively toward common goals. These combinations can help build friendships and mentoring relationships that last even after the semester ends.

One of the most influential forms of social capital is derived from the relationship between a student and a teacher (Brooks 2011; Delpit 2006; Hollins and Guzman 2005). Learning communities provide multiple levels of interaction for students and faculty and allow for more engagement, which often leads to enhanced social capital. Students "not only learn from a teacher but also for a teacher" if the emotional connection is there (Delpit 2006, 227). The learning community provided the opportunity to strengthen existing relationships and to build new connections.

José María, an ESL student who participated in the three-way learning community, faced both cultural pressures and family tragedy when attending college. The bonds he formed with students and faculty helped him through an extremely painful and challenging time in his life and allowed him to accumulate social and cultural capital that he still draws on today.

He confided that growing up as a gay Mexican boy was extremely difficult. Throughout his childhood, he knew that being homosexual was not something to be proud of in his culture because "in everything you hear, either from your family, or from your teachers, or from your friends—homosexuality is never seen as a good thing."

José María was surprised that when he finally revealed his secret to his loving parents, they were confused but became quite supportive. At that time he thought he had overcome the greatest personal challenge in his life, but shortly after graduating from high school and enrolling at El Paso Community College, his mother became very ill. His father had to work long hours to pay the mounting medical bills for treatments in far-off Mexican cities and José María took on new responsibilities such as caring for his disabled sister, cooking family meals, visiting the hospital, and working along with going to school.

He turned to his inner faith for resort, and while his mother was in a coma, he avidly read her scriptures from the Bible. His mother miraculously recovered, and to this day she often asks him "How do you cope with all of it?" José María replies, "¡*No mas no te sueltes del de arriba* [Just don't let go of the Almighty]! That is why I try to see the good in everything, every problem, every bad situation, every struggle, in every moment!"

The learning community played a tremendous role in easing his pain. Through that period of intense stress and suffering, his peers and teachers comforted him, encouraged him, and kept him on track. His relationship with Ms. Rose Galindo, his ESL reading professor, was particularly important. José María described her as a passionate, outspoken, and idealistic teacher.

Not only did she guide him through his studies, but she also helped him work through many of the bigger questions in his life. He believed that like a resourceful medical practitioner, Ms. Galindo could look straight into her students' eyes and diagnose their innermost yearnings and needs. She then prescribed the perfect literary work that would not only alleviate their suffering, but would also help transform their lives.

The learning community members built close relations with each other. Teachers provided great emotional and psychological support and motivated students to succeed. Ms. Galindo pushed them hard at times. She not only immersed the students in stimulating literary discussions and meaningful assignments to ensure in-depth understanding of the readings, but also insisted that the students keep up in their other courses.

It was difficult to fall behind in one class without being noticed. In a firm and paternal way, Ms. Galindo repeatedly checked in with the students and asked, "Hey! Did you have problems understanding anything? Do you have any homework? How are you doing in your other classes?" Ms. Galindo's warm, drill sergeant approach left no room for excuses. You simply had to do the work.

As the students built social capital and were better connected to their peers and teachers, they became more comfortable discussing controversial topics or challenging an idea. They were also able to make the transition to Anglo-American culture in their studies and develop new interests in both of their worlds at once. José María enthusiastically shares the following story:

> Ms. Galindo is great! I really trust her, and so I would ask her, "Do you know what would help me out to cope with this or to understand this better?" I would ask her about everything, and I kept reading and reading and reading until now—thanks to her. She made me realize that I had to make this switch in my

reading because I love to read—and I usually read certain authors in Spanish. She would say, "Try this book in English and this and this." And now I have a whole shelf filled with books in English!

In her work with the ESL students in the learning community, Ms. Galindo played the role of a *cultural translator* (de Anda 1984), a person who is from the student's native culture but who helps bridge the gap between the native world and the mainstream world. She was able to validate José María's love for Spanish literature while gently easing his passion into English language books. Ms. Galindo helped to weave his "passions and intellectual life into one recognizable whole" (Belenky et al. 1986, 141).

Working with Ms. Galindo inspired a lifelong love for learning that helped José María ease into coursework at the University of Texas at El Paso, where the direct relationships of the learning community were often lacking. But he had already built some of the social and cultural capital needed to survive there. He understood the process required for improved learning now, and he was able to make use of support services such as counseling or tutoring whenever he was falling behind. He felt an obligation to succeed because of all that the community college had invested in him through its faculty, staff, and students. José María had not only learned *from* Ms. Galindo but was also learning *for* Ms. Galindo (Delpit 2006).

José María has graduated from the University of Texas at El Paso with a bachelor's degree but continues to make use of his acquired capital both at EPCC and at the university. He recently returned and visited his teachers at the community college and enthusiastically received letters of recommendation for entrance into the master's program in social work.

Abigail also built social and cultural capital through the learning community. Her family immigrated to the United States when she was a teenager, and she and her brother attended a high school in Dallas, Texas. They were the only students from Mexico and, even though Abigail was proud of her Mexican heritage, she was keenly aware that not being fluent in English was a major barrier. For years, her family moved back and forth between Mexico and different cities in the United States, and she never quite got the chance to master the language.

Even though she dreamed of getting a college degree someday, cultural traditions were often a barrier. She had been married for years and had a fairly traditional relationship with her husband. When she raised the subject of school at home, her husband repeatedly told her that "we don't have the money and you have to be at home with the kids and you need to help me with my business." Despite the challenges, at the age of thirty-eight, Abigail entered the ESL program at El Paso Community College and enrolled in the learning community. She took a student loan and tried to balance the role of a traditional Mexican wife with that of an ambitious, nontraditional college student.

The learning community provided her with an opportunity to build social capital in classes, capital that she had been unable to acquire in high school or because of moving from city to city, crossing borders, and living in between cultures. In college, she developed new relationships with teachers, relationships that had been impossible before. This type of simple engagement can make a major difference in a student's chances for success.

For example, in a study of high school students, researchers found that they could predict with a high level of accuracy which students were going to drop out by simply asking them about the types of relationships they have with their teachers (Sroufe et al. 2005). Most of those who dropped out never connected or built bridges with their teachers (Sroufe et al. 2005). The college environment often makes these connections even less attainable; however, learning communities encourage this type of engagement, motivation, and stimulation.

Abigail's community college teachers introduced her to new ways of understanding. Because she felt comfortable in the learning community, she was more confident and more open during discussions. One topic that generated great interest in her Education 1300 class was that of social reproduction theory and its link to success. The students were surprised at how people born into poverty tended to remain in poverty throughout their lives and how people born into the middle or upper classes tended to do the same. There was much less mobility than they had imagined.

Yet they also saw that many people were able to move up, join the middle class, and live a comfortable life. Taking classes or getting a degree was important, but it did not necessarily translate into social or economic success. They were amazed at how much of the theory, readings, writing assignments, and discussions about social capital were relevant to their situation. They began to see that through social and cultural capital the cycle could be broken.

The learning community motivated Abigail to continue with her studies. Her new relationships with others provided tremendous support. For example, she and many of her fellow ESL students had heard horror stories about entering traditional college classes in which faculty had much less contact with the students. The teachers seemed to be involved in other matters, spent less time on campus, and were essentially disconnected. Some spoke of large university lecture halls in which students seldom have a chance to interact with professors at all.

The learning community showed that it did not necessarily have to be that way and that the students probably did not understand the need for more interaction with faculty until they experienced it for themselves. Abigail noted, "I think it is important to take the time to talk to the teachers." She cited the example of Dr. Myshie Pagel, her ESL writing professor, who offered students time for tutoring and advising, help that Abigail viewed as an important tool in building her academic career.

> Abigail: Dr. Pagel wrote the tutoring schedule on the board but nobody showed up! I know she was focusing on the ones that were getting low grades, but nobody showed up. A friend and I went and were standing outside and we asked her, "Do you have room for us?" She said, "Come on in!"

> Interviewer: I'm sure she was very happy!

> Abigail: Anytime something extra is offered, I will be there! During tutoring the teachers have more time and explain things differently. You have a chance to really talk to them. It is important for many reasons, so I will make time to be there.

Abigail is consciously and unconsciously aware that Dr. Pagel's meeting is about more than just tutoring and that this encounter has the potential of yielding social capital. She and other students were often amazed at how few students took advantage of, or even understood the significance of, these interactions. Abigail began to understand the value of these encounters, and she now encourages her children to do the same with their teachers. She said: "I always tell my kids, 'When something extra is offered you go for it because you don't know what it could turn into!'"

In Abigail's perception of mainstream culture the "extras" have a certain value and are a form of social capital. Relationships in these professional settings are vital for this group of students because they can generate various forms of capital that are not typically within reach. These new social networks with faculty provide a window into a different aspect of the college, the faculty members' perspectives, and unique opportunities for help. They can lead to other supportive contexts and institutional resources. The learning community made these and other exchanges possible. Several of the students worked with all three faculty members for feedback on research papers or ideas for the projects required for their classes.

Abigail also acquired another exciting form of cultural capital in the learning community: a greater awareness of the world and the ability to discuss current events and broader global ideas with people. Abigail was very impressed with the fact that Dr. Pagel knew what was happening all around the country and even around the world. She described her as a news media correspondent "who knew everything," and she soon grew to find Dr. Pagel's enthusiasm for worldly knowledge, historical events, and women's issues contagious. She started to watch the news every night and made a concerted effort to learn more about current events in order to prepare for classroom discussions.

When Dr. Pagel began her class by asking, "So what is happening in the news today?" Abigail was ready for action. She had sparked a great interest in the world among her students, was successful in getting them involved in learning, and whetted their appetite for more knowledge. The new knowledge as well as the validation Abigail received by participating in class discussions in the learning community allowed her to more freely interact with her other teachers. As a successful middle-class female, Dr. Pagel was modeling some of the behaviors of the mainstream society and was directly and indirectly assisting Abigail in understanding some of the rules and codes of the dominant culture. She too was playing the role of a *cultural translator* and was paving the way for Abigail to make the transition into a very different world and to build cultural capital (de Anda 1984).

GETTING READY TO MEET THE WORLD

One of the difficulties many students face after acquiring social capital is transforming it into cultural capital. In order to transition into and function in a new academic or professional world, they need to present themselves in interviews, discussions with peers, or formal presentations or speeches. Additionally, they will need to openly demonstrate educational, social, and intellectual knowledge as well as qualifications, skills, and abilities in order to impress an interviewer or land a competitive position. EPCC professor of Speech and Drama Lisa McNiel builds college student resilience by teaching them how to overcome a very common human condition: stage fright.

During one of her lively, creative presentations titled "Fake It 'til You Make It: Acting Your Way to Self-Esteem," she helps her students analyze and conquer their fears, present themselves to the class, and build a strong sense of self-esteem, all of which are essential for resilience.

Lisa is an enthusiastic, dynamic, vibrant speaker with a striking resemblance to the actress Michelle Pfeiffer. Her speech classes are revered and feared, just like college math or physics. She suddenly announces to her pupils, "This is the moment you have been waiting for: Stage Fright!!!!" Everyone in the room is a bit anxious, nervously smiling or laughing with excitement, as McNiel begins her session. She asks for two volunteers to do a role-play exercise. A petite Hispanic female in her early twenties is given the role of a cavewoman and a dark-haired Hispanic male of similar build and age plays the role of a tiger.

They choose their costumes from a table piled with leopard-skinned drapes, multicolored scarves, and a variety of hats and props. McNiel guides the action, coaching the cavewoman as she runs around the room, chased by a tiger that has not eaten in days. When she barely escapes the claws of the tiger, the class breaks into applause. McNiel explains the biological reactions taking place in the cavewoman's brain and body. The students learn that the physiological and psychological symptoms of stage fright are similar to those of an ancient Neanderthal, produced during a syndrome known as "fight or flight."

The class is excited, anxious, and captivated just watching the action. McNiel brings them down with a reading of an article titled "Ways to Calm Your Mind" by two prominent experts in relaxation techniques, Harvard Medical School's Herbert Benson and medical author Julie Corliss. She then takes the class through a progressive relaxation exercise to bring them down and then allows them to see how their minds and bodies are reacting. Once they return to a normal, relaxed state, they are free to move on to their next class.

Lisa McNiel is a kind, compassionate professor who teaches con respeto. She deeply empathizes with her students and understands their fears. She knows that community college students are different from traditional university students and that they may find it personally and culturally uncomfortable to present themselves in public performances. She acknowledges that her background is quite different from that of many students. She is a white female who was raised in a middle-class family of educators.

McNiel's father was a school principal and her mother was a speech therapist. Therefore, from an early age, she had a "frame of reference" or the cultural knowledge required to participate in mainstream society. She says that "our students, on the other hand, tend to be first generation college students and come from diverse backgrounds" and therefore need to learn this new frame of reference.

McNiel believes it is her responsibility to "teach beyond the curriculum" in order to provide students with the knowledge that will help them "survive and thrive in the system." She stated that "effective communication is the most powerful form of social and cultural capital that 'can make you or break you.'" She notes that her department has the highest number of nominees and recipients of the Minnie Stevens Piper Award, a prestigious Texas teaching distinction, not because they are better than the other departments, but "because we have the written and oral communication skills, and when filling out an application we know how to present ourselves on paper. I want students to learn these skills so that they can have access to this power."

McNiel understands that communication is one of the most important competencies a student should acquire. She has experienced firsthand the benefits of this form of cultural capital and as a result found creative ways to help students obtain it. Her understanding of and deep empathy for community college students came from "being in theater where you sort of naturally have to be able to put yourself in other people's places, but I really think part if it comes from my own college experience."

Lisa graduated from El Paso High School as salutatorian and "theoretically was the cream of the crop." She attended Rice University but had experiences similar to a typical community college student:

> Once I faced competitive situations, I really felt like a fish out of water. I didn't know as much as the other students. I wasn't as prepared. I certainly didn't fit into Rice. I felt a strong sense of inferiority. I think my empathy comes from learning techniques to overcome that. I try to put myself in their situations. It also comes from experiences in the past, and just looking at my own life now and trying to survive with a family.

McNiel, an engineering major at the time, ended up dropping several important classes such as physics and chemistry. She earned a C in calculus and laughs as she relates, "I've never been so happy to see a C in my life. I never made C's!" She now tries to teach her students what she wished others would have taught her in order to build the self-esteem she needed to survive at Rice University and later on in life. For this resilient professor, the success of her students is personal.

Lisa is the youngest of three children. Her sister was thirteen and her brother was fifteen when Lisa was born. When Lisa was eight years old, her brother, who was twenty-four years old at the time, committed suicide. She tells the following:

> He was going through a divorce, and it was a bad situation. It was 1972. We didn't have all of these great anti-depressants. There was still a stigma about getting help. It was horrible of course and it tore the family apart. It impacted everything—my childhood, my high school years, my college, my going into the first marriage because I didn't really ever grieve. . . . I was little, and I knew intellectually that he was dead.

Lisa refused to go to the funeral. During most of her childhood, she pretended that her brother was away at college and that he would return for the summer. She waited for years, but he never returned. After a divorce, Lisa received help:

> That was a real struggle, but I'm really glad I went into therapy, and I dealt with that. I looked at myself, and I looked at the issues, and maybe that's where the resilience came from too. Sometimes you have to be willing to dive underneath the surface, and look at it and deal with it. I had to really accept that and let him go. I think that was always sort of a shadow on my back, "Am I going to be him? Is this going to happen to me?"

David Brooks writes that "when most people think about the future, they dream up ways they might live happier lives." But when people are asked to remember events that shaped them, they focus on difficult circumstances they faced. He goes on to say that "most people shoot for happiness but feel formed through suffering" (2015, 93). This is what happened to Lisa. A common finding among resilient individuals is that they learn from their failures and struggles and use these lessons to dramatically change their lives and the lives of others.

When tragedy strikes and the time necessary to grieve has passed, these individuals often "dive underneath the surface" and through a reflective process ask themselves, "What is this experience here to teach me? How do I use this new knowledge to help myself and others?" For McNiel, the answers to these questions or the lessons learned became the pedagogies of survival that allowed her to relate to and teach students in such a remarkable way. Brooks and many others believe that it is often our responses to these struggles that transform our careers into "callings." This was certainly the case for Lisa.

Professor McNiel sees her calling as a servant and encourages her community college students to recognize that they have something important to say. She believes that it is her duty to help build their confidence so that they can say it. She provides students with the strategies and techniques that will allow them to be "more powerful agents in their lives." She paves the way for students by encouraging them, engaging them, and teaching them how to become great communicators so they can truly build cultural capital.

Conclusion

A Resilience Vision

The dreams of Mexican American students can become a reality by cultivating their resilience. At institutions like El Paso Community College, one of the gardens of possibility, professors help foster that resilience by building on personal and environmental factors, teaching *con respeto*, validating students' strengths and abilities, helping them gain a sense of purpose in life, and by creating spaces for engagement in which they can accumulate the social and cultural capital required to thrive in the world.

Many of the teachers draw on their own humble pathways to success, pathways that have allowed them to overcome obstacles, reach their academic goals, and help others do the same. They have much to offer their students and have the ability to make dramatic changes in their lives. Through their own struggles and achievements, they often find that they have the power to strengthen the resilience of others.

Those highlighted in this work do this in many ways. It may be a brief, apparently insignificant action, such as guiding a student to a particular resource or suggesting a new educational direction. It can be a small insight or awareness obtained from their own journey that helped them solve a problem. It may be introducing students to challenging readings and assignments that allow them to learn more about their own worlds. It can happen by being a warm demander or by developing a deeper, long-term relationship as a friend and mentor.

Mexican Americans comprise the largest segment of the Latino population, the fastest-growing and largest minority in the United States today. Mexican American students tend to come from lower-income homes where neither parent attended college or is familiar with the structure and process of higher education. Many are enmeshed in extensive family responsibilities, such as producing extra income or caring for siblings, children, or the elderly. Women are frequently restricted by traditional social roles and are expected to be "good" sisters, wives, and mothers. Limited proficiency in English has often held them back. Many Mexican American students have had fewer opportunities to develop their full potential and many have had little contact with higher education. Entering college for them is like entering the unknown.

Community colleges, the democratic second chance institutions, can help change these circumstances and offer a new, fresh start. They have the potential to create opportunities and advance equality, bringing a large minority population into the mainstream. Latinos are more likely than any other minority group to enroll at a community college and consistently choose these institutions of higher learning over universities. They see these gardens of possibility as a way to seek a better life for themselves and their families.

Community colleges have traditionally been understudied and ignored in much of the literature. Well into the twenty-first century, they continue to be "honored but invisible." Many of the experiences recorded in this book shed light on what happens in these institutions. They show how dedicated faculty can use their own experiences, knowledge, and creativity to learn, teach, engage, and mentor Mexican American students and help them achieve their goals in college and in their lives. Much more study is needed to understand how this process takes place at our second chance institutions.

The study of resilience is a relatively new field in psychology. It is a new paradigm, a shift in thinking, in which the focus is on the wellness of rather than the illness of the individual. Benard describes four basic attributes and explains how each can play a role in developing an individual's resilience. Social competency can help someone communicate better and relate to others in more meaningful, connected ways. Problem-solving and planning skills can help a person develop strategies for dealing with a personal obstacle or reaching a goal.

Resilient individuals develop autonomy, an empowering sense of themselves and an understanding of their potential place in the world. All of this can lead to a better sense of purpose in someone's life. A resilient person does not necessarily need to develop all of these characteristics in equal measures or at the same time to achieve success. Even small changes can often produce significant results.

By building on these personal protective factors, Mexican American college students can advance further. They can focus on long-term goals, become more mindful in their daily lives, discover their elements, be more organized and driven in their work, have a larger sense of purpose, and ultimately achieve happiness.

Environmental factors can also contribute greatly to success, especially the support of families. Most of the families featured in this book did not have the financial resources to help their children directly, but they offered other valuable forms of support. They provided knowledge and inspiration often in the form of oral traditions such as *consejos*, *dichos*, and stories. *"El ignorate grita, el inteligente opina, pero el sabio calla"* (The ignorant person yells, the intelligent one gives his or her opinion, but the wise one remains silent) was commonly heard in Mexican American homes. This inspired these students to humbly work hard and achieve success.

Meaningful experiences in school and engagement in their communities can also provide a solid foundation. Participating in community activities through college often led to new interests and pursuits.

Studying and interacting with enthusiastic, intellectually curious teachers can add even further to this process. Teacher quality certainly plays an important role. Again and again students glowingly spoke of the wide breadth of knowledge and intellectual curiosity possessed by many of their teachers. They reported that their professors often had a deep sustained interest in their experiences and studies. These resilient teachers understood the process of self-discovery. They encouraged critical inquiries, developed creative assignments, and set higher standards. This caused many students to learn "for" their teachers as well as learn "from" their teachers.

Teaching con respeto can build on a student's personal and environmental protective factors. This approach to teaching sees possibilities in all students and establishes high expectations in a nurturing but demanding educational environment. A professor can enter the student's world and explore and honor his or her inherent personal and cultural knowledge. Teaching con respeto cultivates relationships, connecting students to a new world of professionals and academics. Both the teacher and the student can be role models for each other, building off of each others' abilities and ambitions.

The teacher can enter the student's world and make curriculum and assignments meaningful and relevant. Teachers can "make it real." Joe Old's community studies open students' eyes and reveal a world they live in but have never really understood. Students learn that their challenges are often part of a universal drama and can learn from studying other people's struggles and triumphs. Myshie Pagel and Rose Galindo help them explore the challenges of racism, machismo, gender roles, and economic structures.

Pagel and Galindo delved even further by exposing racial ideologies that exist in the students' own Mexican heritage, ideologies that many were unaware of or in some cases strongly denied. This put other concepts about race in context. It allowed the teachers to enter an often unvisited area of the students' world and promote deep, critical thinking. Students like Robert were able to build on their cultural roots. He drew on his childhood summers in Las Huertas to better understand his heritage and family traditions. Crista drew on similar experiences. Teaching con respeto can be the gateway to a more inclusive style of instruction, one that encompasses the students' world, allows for more reflection, and expands their thinking.

The process of validation can play an extremely important role. It can help community college students confirm that they are part of a college culture and can help them develop their aptitudes and abilities to succeed in higher education. The EPCC faculty validate many of these students' experiences by encouraging them to learn about themselves. They help them identify their strengths, work toward goals, and develop an enhanced confidence. In this way, students can break cycles and experience a sense of progress. The process of validation can heighten self-awareness and autonomy, which are important aspects of resilience.

The first-year experience course can play a critical role in validating a student. While presenting a basic introduction to the world of college, it can also provide students with many tools for self-analysis. For many community college students, this is the first time they are able to learn so much about their skills, aptitudes, and personalities.

The first-year experience course introduces new ideas, concepts, and approaches. It shows how elements of educational psychology can help a freshman student forge a pathway through future studies and careers. The course can lead him or her on a journey of personal growth and professional exploration. By studying the works of Jung, Maslow, and Lyubomirsky, he or she can discover his or her inner self, identify strengths and weaknesses, validate his or her abilities, and plan new strategies for the future.

Simple inventories can open entirely new worlds for the student, revealing some areas that are well grounded and others that need some attention. Under the guidance of a master teacher like Lolo Mercado, the course can integrate educational psychology, counseling methods, self-awareness, and basic skills enhancement, all of which are essential to building resilience.

Learning communities can also provide firm validation. Cooperative ventures, paired courses, and the creation of new spaces for interaction and exploration can validate students further. They can bond by addressing common problems such as language, gender, and culture. Learning communities can lead to a much closer engagement with faculty than is possible in a typical college course. They allow for direct, personal connections with professionals who sometimes serve as cultural mediators or translators and may potentially become role models or mentors.

Once validated, students can focus on their larger purposes in college and in their lives.

As students are taught con respeto, are validated, and build autonomy, they often discover that they are a part of something larger than themselves. The pursuit of a college degree starts as a personal goal but soon evolves into something broader and more inclusive. Resilient students find that they become more connected to their families, peers, and communities. They begin to understand that college will allow them to elevate their family members along with them, they can lift as they climb, and they can steer their lives and the lives of others in entirely new directions.

As these students cultivate a larger purpose, they begin to see their educational experiences as a way to truly change history for future generations. These student experiences might help end cycles of abandonment, change gender relations in their family, or create new role models for their brothers, sisters, or children. Crista developed a new dedication and commitment to children and took on the role of a teacher while still being a student. She extended that role to other students, helped her peers succeed, and led her own family in new directions. As she learned to read and develop critical thinking skills, she became an activist in her community.

Sofía's eye-opening service learning project in the deaf community introduced her to a world that few have ever entered and led her to organize her fellow students to rescue a client in dire need of help. Richard Yañez and the Puente Project play a vital role in the lives of Mexican American students and help develop new generations of *puentistas*, who can lead their communities in the future.

Throughout all of these processes, Mexican American community college students can acquire social and cultural capital. As they engage in new relationships with teachers, members of the community, and other professionals, they make connections and venture further out into the world. Over time they build up reserves that can be used to access new projects, help them with admission to competitive programs, or enter a profession after graduation.

Social and cultural capital can lead them into an unfamiliar world, a middle-class, professional world in which a different culture exists. They can learn the rules and play the game. This allows them to comfortably interact with people from different educational, economic, ethnic, and social backgrounds. Their social competency develops further and they can then enter Stanton-Salazar's "social freeway," where they can use their capital to move more smoothly through the system and achieve their goals.

But Mexican American community college students do not necessarily have to abandon their culture to acquire social and cultural capital. Instead they can balance respeto with ambition and find a middle ground. This allows them to engage more with faculty and other professionals, often leading to a mentoring relationship. This is particularly important for women, who often have more responsibilities at home and fewer role models. A deeper understanding of the rules and comfortable engagement with faculty can help them maintain much of their cultural integrity while achieving their goals. With the guidance of teachers like Ms. Lisa McNiel, they can learn to present themselves to the world.

As a major second chance institution in a thriving borderland community, El Paso Community College serves as a garden of possibility, nurturing its students, helping them become resilient, and sending them off to pursue a greater purpose in their own lives and the world. As EPCC and other community colleges cultivate the resilience of Mexican American students, they not only help the individuals succeed, but also help develop a new generation of leaders. These resilient students can overcome barriers and move on to university studies, become role models and agents of change for their families, play more active roles in their communities, enter professions in larger numbers, make valuable contributions to our society, and ultimately achieve their dreams, an essential part of the greater American Dream.

Appendix

Critical Resilience

The theoretical perspective of critical resilience emerged as a result of reflection on data gathered from three studies of Mexican American students and one study of professors at El Paso Community College over an eight-year period. The stories told by community college students and professors were often layered and complex, just like my own. What became clear was that capturing the true spirit of how these students and professors overcame obstacles and persisted would require digging below the surface of the current literature on resilience and studying the larger contexts of the social, cultural, economic, and historical aspects of schooling.

It became apparent that without carefully considering the structures of schooling and mainstream society many questions remained unanswered and the dynamics of power embedded in these systems were still unexamined (Campa 2010). Without considering these larger systems, we run the risk of attributing success and failure to the individual and relieving educational institutions and our greater society of responsibility, thus continuing to perpetuate the status quo.

In order to see more precisely how individuals, especially Mexican American community college students, build resilience, we need to question power dynamics within a social and cultural context. How do we do this? The poet Audre Lorde (1997) offers some insight into this topic. She reminds us that as we work, "the master's tools will never dismantle the master's house." Therefore I borrowed a few tools and a few principles from feminism and critical theory, including context, power, knowledge, and relationships. I may not dismantle the house, but I am engaged in some serious renovations.

THE IMPORTANCE OF CONTEXT

González, Moll, and Amanti (2005) write about the importance of looking at an individual's experiences within larger contexts. Learning "does not just take place 'between the ears' but is eminently a social process" (ix). Many Latina and black feminists use a critical theoretical perspective to view macro structures, or larger social, political, and economical constraints, as obstacles that keep students from achieving success (Villenas et al. 2006). Valenzuela (1999) explains that many schools are organized in ways that "fracture students' cultural and ethnic identities" and create divisions between the students and the staff (5).

Instead many Latina and black feminists promote schooling and education that is centered on wholeness or a holistic interconnection of spirit, mind, and body in relation to family and friends, school, communities, and society (González 2001). They challenge traditional patriarchal knowledge and power and give voice to the experiences of marginalized communities.

In other words, they extend the meaning of education far beyond the school setting and value and promote knowledge that is not necessarily part of the mainstream culture. For Mexican American students, language, family, cultural background, and socioeconomic status are often viewed as "deficits" or deficiencies and are used to justify academic failure (Valenzuela 1999; Valdés 1996; Nieto 2004). The argument is made that if students have mainstream language, family structure, cultural background, and higher socioeconomic status, they would be much more likely to succeed.

I argue that resilience needs to be reconceptualized to focus on the strengths that Mexican American students bring to the community college and how those strengths offer alternate pathways for success. In order to understand these strengths, there needs to be a new way of looking at the data. With feminist critical influence and the basic framework of resilience theory, we can analyze narratives for their social, cultural, economic, and historical contexts.

With this new critical resilience lens, we can do the work of "excavation," asking questions about power, knowledge, and relationships, and can add important new dimensions to our broader understanding of Mexican American community college resilience (Delgado Bernal 1998; DeVault 1996; Hughes 2002; Lipman 1998; Maher and Tetreault 2001). A significant discovery made with the new lens was that students often learned important lessons and developed their own "pedagogies" through their unique cultural experiences. These pedagogies or lessons have helped them build resilience and survive in an unfamiliar world that usually does not recognize their knowledge (Campa 2013a). These "pedagogies of survival" are revealed when the critical resilience lens along with its tools are used to dig deeper and examine underlying layers and intersections.

THE DYNAMICS OF POWER, KNOWLEDGE, AND RELATIONSHIPS

Feminists examine power and privilege in education in order to promote equity, access, and democratic participation (Fine 1994; Shapiro 1992; Ropers-Huilman 1998). They argue that these lofty goals can only be achieved by understanding how power is exercised among and in between groups. Educational systems simply reflect broader structures that are present in mainstream society, such as gender, race, ethnicity, or class, and educational ideologies that have tended to support these structures.

Delpit (1995) detailed an educational "culture of power" in which there are rules or "codes" for participation, rules created by those in power. These could be as simple as the prevalence of bias in staffing or as complex as systems that track students into roles determined by gender or ethnicity. Some students in this study understood the rules that are in place and learned to "play the game" in order to succeed and thrive in a coded environment.

In feminist critical research, questions originate from a woman's perspective. A common conclusion is that, overall, men set the educational agenda and created a system that preserves male dominance and a male understanding of knowledge. Historically, men have decided what knowledge is important to know and how to use it. Feminists tend to question or query knowledge by looking at how knowledge is obtained, by whom, and for what purpose.

This same questioning can be applied to the context of Mexican American students functioning in a white-dominated educational system. Whose knowledge is the system based on and whose knowledge is being left out? In a pluralistic society, rather than a traditional "melting pot," it is important that each subgroup maintain its identity, heritage, and values, and that those values be reflected in the broader social processes such as education (Broido and Manning 2002).

Feminists emphasize how relationships play an important role in learning, human development, and moral reasoning and, I would add, success (Shapiro 1992). Two important "relational resources" that some Mexican American students have accessed are known as social and cultural capital. The "capital" consists of resources that are acquired, spent, or invested. Like our everyday use of money, a person who does not understand the value of money may squander it and quickly deplete his or her reserves. A money-conscious person learns how to best make use of it, save it, invest it, and utilize it for bigger purposes.

Stanton-Salazar (2004) explains how social capital can be acquired and used to obtain cultural capital. He makes an analogy with currency: some students come to school with U.S. dollars while others come with Mexican pesos. The pesos, while useful in another culture, are devalued, while the dollars, the standard of the mainstream culture, hold their weight.

In other words, even though both groups of students come with knowledge and experiences, educational institutions are designed in ways that discount or even negate social capital from the nondominant culture. Stanton-Salazar's (2004) currency metaphor helps to explain how educational systems reproduce the distribution of cultural capital among different groups of people. Therefore academic achievement must extend far beyond simple performance. It needs to allow for and cultivate relationships and interactions with those who have access to this capital. Social and cultural capital are crucial in the educational resilience of Mexican Americans who attend community colleges.

Feminist critical theory emphasizes the importance of context, power, knowledge, and relationships in educational structures and society that can overlap and intersect each other (DeVault 1996; Reinharz 1992). Community college students often inhabit multiple intersections. For example, they tend to be older, female, Latino, and are in the process of learning a second language. Collins (2000) reminds us that intersections of race, gender, class, sexuality, culture, language, and other social identities cannot be reduced to just one identity because they work together to produce various injustices. The opposite is also true. Intersections of social identities can serve as powerful protective factors that cultivate resilience.

USING A CRITICAL RESILIENCE LENS

In one study, two female students who were raised in working-class Mexican immigrant families questioned and resisted machismo and patriarchal traditions in both Mexican and American cultures. Sofía and Crista saw how these traditions stifled their mothers, restricting their lives despite the fact that they were talented and ambitious.

> Sofía: I think my mom could have been. . . . She has so many qualities but because of my dad and the machismo and certain things, she did not pursue what she wanted to do. And I see so many good qualities in her!

> Crista: I think our mothers are great. My mother was not the best mother, but she had very interesting talents, and we have to be fair and acknowledge that. My mother was college material! And she was learning algebra when she was 7 years old, and she was in the school house. There were just things that brought her down. . . . Like my father.

The questioning of power brought agency. Rather than simply blaming their mothers, fathers, or culture, they chose to disrupt traditional beliefs and change their own destinies and those of their children. They "dreamed of possibilities beyond those of their mothers' lives" (Villenas and Moreno 2001, 675). Sofía's and Crista's actions revealed that they were determined to resist and interrupt this history, and this determination of theirs allowed them to achieve success at EPCC. They often talked about how important it was to show their children *que sí se puede* (that yes, it can be done)!

Many female students at El Paso Community College understand that their mothers were resilient and had the capacities and the personal protective factors needed for academic success; however, imposed cultural beliefs greatly limited their success. Through the sharply focused lens of critical resilience, we can see the larger context and can now understand how Sofía and Crista, and probably many others, used history as a motivational force. Morales (2013) wrote that "the depth and profundity of the lessons we learn and knowledge we gain (as well as the impact we can then have on others) are commensurate with the severity of the traumas we endure" (65).

Sofía's and Crista's stories are only a few examples of the treasures that can be found when a deficit perspective is replaced with a critical resilience perspective. Rather than simply seeing the two women as outliers, they can be brought into sharper focus against a background of society and culture. This type of critical resilience examination reveals what I call pedagogies of survival.

METHODS

Purposeful sampling was used to select the participants for these qualitative studies on resilience. Merriam (1998) explains that purposeful sampling "is based on the assumption that the investigator wants to discover, understand, and gain insight, and therefore, must select a sample from which the most can be learned" (61). In order to learn how students use their resilience to navigate through educational structures, it was important to select those who had already successfully maneuvered their way through these systems. Therefore the studies included some students with several intersections who had dropped out of EPCC and later returned, or ones who had struggled with their coursework initially but were now in their third semester and had managed to maintain a good GPA of 3.0 or higher.

In order to locate potential participants, I spoke with faculty members from various disciplines. We discussed some of the research on resilience, and I emphasized that I was not looking for "honor students," but was instead searching for students who faced difficult circumstances because of their multiple intersections and negotiated their adversity in ways that helped them achieve success. In addition, I gave these colleagues very specific criteria required for the study. For example, the two most important criteria were that the students be of Mexican origin and have been raised in working-class homes.

In order to meet these two criteria, the participants' parent/s had to be of Mexican origin, with neither parent completing college while the participant was growing up. Other intersections such as age or learning English as a second language were also included. As Delgado Bernal (1998) notes, language is often used to marginalize Mexican Americans. All student participants were guaranteed anonymity. Pseudonyms unrelated to their real names were used throughout.

The professor participants were nominated by students who were asked to write responses to two questions. The first question asked the students to name a professor who they considered to be a "great teacher," and the second question asked them to explain specifically what the professor did that "made him or her great." I selected those who were nominated several times and exhibited personal and environmental protective factors. Once I narrowed the list, I focused on those who had either impacted the student in meaningful ways or had perhaps fostered their resilience. I selected professors from various subject areas. All the professors opted to use their real names, with the exception of one faculty member who requested and was granted a pseudonym.

The primary data collection process involved student and professor interviews, which Merriam (2009) cites as the best technique to use when "conducting intensive case studies of a few selected individuals" (88). It can reveal "how people interpret the world around them" (88). Interviews allow us "to enter into the other person's perspective" (Patton 2002, 340–41). A questionnaire was created to generate discussions and semistructured interviews were conducted using a protocol that addressed themes related to resilience, teaching and learning, academic achievement, family, culture, and language (Merriam 2009).

The student and professor participants were interviewed at least once in a location of their choice and the length of time varied from one to three hours. A second data collection strategy involved written documentation, forms or documents that were not gathered through observations or interviews (Merriam 2009). Some examples were class assignments, such as reflective papers, or summaries and analyses of the materials read and discussed in class and notes from presentations. A third data collection technique included classroom observations. The research processes were reviewed and approved by EPCC's Institutional Review Board.

The author taught the Education 1300 course in the three-way learning community (the third study). Therefore her role as professor and researcher automatically made her a participant-observer in the study. This "comingling of roles" brings to the forefront the issue of subjectivity, which is "a common occurrence in anthropological fieldwork" and qualitative case studies such as this one (Ladson-Billings 2001, 145). Becoming integrated in the study was necessary in order to enter into the participants' worlds, teach them, and learn from them while utilizing a critical resilience framework. I engaged in ongoing self-conscious reflection about my role in the study by documenting my observations, thoughts, and reactions in a researcher's journal (Zavella 1997).

I examined how I was "situated within [the] social and power relations" of my work with the participants, my colleagues, and the college setting (Zavella 1997, 45). In addition, I engaged in an inductive process that involved working back and forth among themes and data while collaborating with the participants so that they had an opportunity to shape the themes as they emerged from the research process (Creswell 2007). The analysis was an ongoing process and the data was coded and triangulated for themes (Merriam 2009). This was done for each participant and across all the sources of data using a critical resilience lens. These measures were set in place to ensure the studies were conducted in a trustworthy manner that respected, honored, and reflected the participants' views without overrepresenting the researcher's personal perspectives (Arminio and Hultgren 2002).

References

Albom, M. 1997. *Tuesdays with Morrie: An Old Man, a Young Man, and Life's Greatest Lesson.* New York: Broadway Books.

Anderson, J. A. 2004. "Academic and Social Integration: A Key to First-Year Success for Students of Color." In *Transforming the First Year of College for Students of Color* (Monograph No. 38), edited by L. I. Rendón, M. García, and D. Person, 77–89. Columbia, SC: University of South Carolina, National Resource Center for the First-Year Experience and Students in Transition.

Arminio, J. L., and F. H. Hultgren. 2002. "Breaking Out from the Shadow: The Question of Criteria in Qualitative Research." *Journal of College Student Development* 43 (4): 424–45.

Bailey, T., D. Jenkins, and T. Leinback. 2005, June. "Is Student Success Labeled Institutional Failure?: Student Goal and Graduation Rates in the Accountability Debate at Community Colleges" (CCRC Working Paper No. 1). New York: Columbia University, Teachers College, Community College Research Center.

Baily, T., and V. S. Morrest. 2006. "Introduction." In *Defending the Community College Equity Agenda*, edited by T. Baily and V. S. Morrest, 1–27. Baltimore, MD: John Hopkins University Press.

Bandura, A. 1997. *Self-Efficacy: The Exercise of Control.* New York: W. H. Freeman.

Barefoot, B. O., and P. P. Fidler. 1996. *The National Survey of Freshmen Seminar Programs: Continuing Innovations in the Collegiate Curriculum.* Columbia, SC: University of South Carolina, National Resource Center for the First-Year Experience and Students in Transition.

Barefoot, B. O., and J. N. Gardner. 1993. "The Freshmen Orientation Seminar: Extending the Benefits of Traditional Orientation." In *Designing Successful Transitions: A Guide for Orienting Students to College* (Monograph No. 13), edited by M. L. Upcraft et al., 141–53. Columbia, SC: University of South Carolina, National Resource Center for the First-Year Experience and Students in Transition.

Belenky, M. F., B. M. Clinchy, N. R. Goldberger, and J. M. Tarule. 1986. *Women's Ways of Knowing: The Development of Self, Voice, and Mind.* New York: Basic Books.

Belsky, J. 2013. *Experiencing the Lifespan*, third edition. New York: Worth Publishers.

Benard, B. 1993. "Fostering Resiliency in Kids." *Educational Leadership* 51 (3): 44–48.

———. 2004. *Resiliency: What We Have Learned.* San Francisco, CA: WestEd.

———. 2007. "Putting the Strengths-Based Approach into Practice: An Interview with Dennis Saleebey, D.S.W." In *Resiliency in Action*, edited by N. Henderson, B. Benard, and N. Sharp-Light, 117–21. Ojai, CA: Resiliency in Action Inc.

Blundo, R. 2006. "Shifting Our Habits of Mind: Learning to Practice from a Strengths Perspective." In *The Strengths Perspective in Social Work Practice*, fourth edition, edited by D. Saleebey, 25–45. New York: Pearson Allyn and Bacon.

Bollati, A. 2006. "To Be Taken for Granted." In *Perspectives on Community College ESL: Vol. 2. Students, Mission, and Advocacy*, edited by C. Machado and A. Blumenthal, 71–85. Alexandria, VA: Teachers of English to Speakers of Other Languages, Inc.

Bransford, J., L. Darling-Hammond, and P. LePage. 2005. "Introduction." In *Preparing Teachers for a Changing World: What Teachers Should Know and Be Able to Do*, edited by L. Darling-Hammond and J. Bransford, 1–39. San Francisco, CA: Jossey-Bass.

Broido, E. M., and K. Manning. 2002. "Philosophical Foundations and Current Theoretical Perspectives in Qualitative Research." *Journal of College Student Development* 43 (4): 434–45.

Brooks, D. 2011. *The Social Animal: The Hidden Sources of Love, Character, and Achievement*. New York: Random House.

———. 2015. *The Road to Character*. New York: Random House.

Cammarota, J. 2004. "The Gendered and Racialized Pathways of Latina and Latino Youth: Different Struggles, Different Resistances in the Urban Context." *Anthropology and Education Quarterly* 35 (1): 53–74. http://dx.doi.org/10.1525/aeq.2004.35.1.53.

Campa, B. 2010. "Critical Resilience, Schooling Processes, and the Academic Success of Mexican Americans in a Community College." *Hispanic Journal of Behavioral Sciences* 32 (3): 429–55. http://dx.doi.org/10.1177/0739986310369322.

———. 2013a. "Pedagogies of Survival: Cultural Resources to Foster Resilience among Mexican-American Community College Students." *Community College Journal of Research and Practice* 37 (4–6): 433–52. http://dx.doi.org/10.1080/10668921003609350.

———. 2013b. "Cultivating Critical Resilience among Hispanic Community College Students through a Three-Way Learning Community." *Journal of Educational and Developmental Psychology* 3 (2): 74–88. http://dx.doi.org/10.5539/jedp.v3n2p74.

Carlson, S. 2014, May 6. "A Caring Professor May Be Key in How a Graduate Thrives." *The Chronicle of Higher Education*. Retrieved March 12, 2016 from http://chronicle.com/article/A-Caring-Professor-May-Be-Key/146409/.

Cochran-Smith, M. 2003. "Teaching Quality Matters." *Journal of Teacher Education* 54 (2): 95–98.

Collins, P. H. 2000. *Black Feminist Thought: Knowledge, Consciousness, and the Politics of Empowerment*, second edition. New York: Routledge Press.

Complete College America. 2012, April. *Remediation: Higher Education's Bridge to Nowhere*. Retrieved December 23, 2015 from https://www.insidehighered.com/sites/default/server_files/files/CCA%20Remediation%20ES%20FINAL.pdf.

Cooper, M. A. 2013, March 18. "Community Colleges by the Numbers." *The Hispanic Outlook in Higher Education* 23: 11–14.

Coyle, D. 2009. *The Talent Code: Greatness Isn't Born. It's Grown*. New York: Bantam.

Creswell, J. W. 2007. *Qualitative Inquiry and Research Design: Choosing among Five Approaches*. Thousand Oaks, CA: Sage Publications.

Csikszentmihalyi, M. 1996. *Creativity: Flow and the Psychology of Discovery and Invention*. New York: HarperCollins.

Darling-Hammond, L. 2006. *Powerful Teacher Education: Lessons from Exemplary Programs*. San Francisco, CA: Jossey-Bass.

de Anda, D. 1984. "Bicultural Socialization: Factors Affecting the Minority Experience." *Social Work* 29 (2): 101–7.

Delgado Bernal, D. 1998. "Using a Chicana Feminist Epistemology in Educational Research." *Harvard Educational Review* 68 (4): 555–82.

———. 2006. "*Mujeres* in College: Negotiating Identities and Challenging Educational Norms." In *Chicana/Latina Education in Everyday Life: Feminista Perspectives on Pedagogy and Epistemology*, edited by D. Delgado Bernal, C. A. Elenes, F. E. Godinez, and S. A. Villenas, 77–79. Albany, NY: SUNY Press.

Delgado-Gaitan, C. 1994. "*Consejos*: The Power of Cultural Narratives." *Anthropology and Education Quarterly* 25 (3): 298–316.

Delpit, L. 1995. *Other People's Children: Cultural Conflict in the Classroom.* New York: New Press.

———. 1996. "The Politics of Teaching Literate Discourse." In *City Kids, City Teachers: Reports from the Front Row*, edited by W. Ayers and P. Ford, 194–208. New York: New Press.

———. 2002. "No Kinda Sense." In *The Skin That We Speak: Thoughts on Language and Culture in the Classroom*, edited by L. Delpit and J. Kilgour Dowdy, 31–48. New York: New Press.

———. 2006. "Lessons from Teachers." *Journal of Teacher Education* 57: 220–31. http://dx.doi.org/10.1177/0022487105285966.

———. 2012. *"Multiplication Is for White People": Raising Expectations for Other People's Children.* New York: New Press.

Denzin, N. K., and Y. S. Lincoln. 2000. "Introduction: The Discipline and Practice of Qualitative Research." In *Handbook of Qualitative Research*, second edition, edited by N. K. Denzin and Y. S. Lincoln, 1–28. Thousand Oaks, CA: Sage Publications.

DeVault, M. 1996. "Talking Back to Sociology: Distinctive Contributions of Feminist Methodology." *Annual Review of Sociology* 22: 29–50.

Dweck, C. S. 2006. *Mindset: The New Psychology of Success: How We Can Learn to Fulfill Our Potential.* New York: Ballantine Books.

Eisner, E. W. 2002. "The Kind of Schools We Need." *Phi Delta Kappan* 83 (8): 576–83.

El Paso Community College. 2010. *Fact Book for 2007–2008 and 2008–2009.* Retrieved on September 25, 2011 from http://www.EPCC.edu.

———. 2011. *President's Message.* Retrieved on September 26, 2011 from http://www.EPCC.edu.

Ennis, S. R., M. Rio-Vargas, and N. G. Albert. 2011. "The Hispanic Population 2010: 2010 Census Briefs." *United States Census Bureau.* Retrieved on April 13, 2013 from http://www.census.gov/prod/cen2010/briefs/c2010br-04.pdf.

Ferguson, R. F. 1991. "Paying for Public Education: New Evidence on How and Why Money Matters." *Harvard Journal on Legislation* 28 (2): 465–98.

Ferrett, S. K. 2015. *Peak Performance: Success in College and Beyond*, ninth edition. New York: McGraw-Hill.

Fine, M. 1994. "Dis-tance and Other Stances: Negotiations of Power Inside Feminist Research." In *Power and Method: Political Activism and Educational Research*, edited by A. Gitlin, 13–35. New York: Routledge.

Fordham, S., and J. U. Ogbu. 1986. "Black Students School Success: Coping with the 'Burden of Acting White.'" *Urban Review* 18 (3): 176–206. http://dx.doi.org/10.1007/BF01112192.

Fosdick, H. E. 1958, November 17. "Fosdick to King." Papers 4: 536–37.

Fry, R. 2002. *Latinos in Higher Education: Many Enroll Too Few Graduate.* Washington, DC: Pew Hispanic Center. Retrieved May 17, 2007 from http://www.pewhispanic.org/site/docs/pdf/latinosinhighereducation.

Gándara, P. 1995. *Over the Ivy Walls: The Educational Mobility of Low-Income Chicanos.* Albany, NY: SUNY Press.

———. 2002. "Meeting Common Goals: Linking K–12 and College Interventions." In *Increasing Access to College: Extending Possibilities for All Students*, edited by W. G. Tierney and L. S. Hagedorn, 81–103. Albany, NY: SUNY Press.

———. 2004. "Building Bridges to College." *Educational Leadership* 62 (3): 56–60.

Gardner, H. 1983. *Frames of Mind: The Theory of Multiple Intelligences.* New York: Basic Books.

Garza, E., P. Reyes, and E. T. Trueba. 2004. *Resiliency and Success: Migrant Children in the U.S.* Boulder, CO: Paradigm Publishers.

Gibson, M. A., P. Gándara, and J. Peterson Koyama. 2004. "The Role of Peers in the Schooling of U.S. Mexican Youth." In *School Connections: U.S. Mexican Youth and School Achievement*, edited by M. A. Gibson, P. Gándara, and J. Peterson Komaya, 1–13. New York: Teachers College Press.

Gladwell, M. 2008. *Outliers: The Story of Success.* New York: Little, Brown and Co.

González, F. G. 2001. "Haciendo Que Hacer—Cultivating a Mestiza Worldview and Academic Achievement: Braiding Cultural Knowledge into Educational Research, Policy, and Practice." *International Journal of Qualitative Studies in Education* 14 (5): 641–56.

Gonzalez, J. 2009, November 20. "Connecting with Part-Timers Is Key Challenge for Community Colleges, Survey Finds." *The Chronicle of Higher Education*, A19.

González, N. 2001. *I Am My Language: Discourses of Women and Children in the Borderlands.* Tucson, AZ: University of Arizona.

González, N., L. C. Moll, and C. Amanti. 2005. *Funds of Knowledge: Theorizing Practices in Household Communities and Classrooms.* Mahwah, NJ: Lawrence Erlbaum Associates, Inc.

Gonzalez, R., and A. M. Padilla. 1997. "The Academic Resilience of Mexican American High School Students." *Hispanic Journal of Behavioral Sciences* 19 (3): 301–17.

Greitens, E. 2015. *Resilience: Hard-Won Wisdom for Living a Better Life.* New York: Houghton Mifflin Harcourt.

Grubb, W. N., et al. 1999. *Honored but Invisible: An Inside Look at Teaching in Community Colleges.* New York: Routledge.

Haggerty, R. J., L. R. Sherrod, N. Garmezy, and M. Rutter. 1994. *Stress, Risk, and Resilience in Children and Adolescents: Process, Mechanisms, and Interventions.* Cambridge, UK: Cambridge University Press.

Hassinger, M., and L. A. Plourde. 2005. "Beating the Odds: How Bi-Lingual Hispanic Youth Work through Adversity to Become High Achieving Students." *Education* 126 (2): 316–27.

Henderson, N. 2012. *The Resiliency Workbook: Bounce Back Stronger, Smarter, and with Real Self-Esteem.* Solvang, CA: Resiliency in Action Inc.

Hollins, E. R., and M. T. Guzman. 2005. "Research on Preparing Teachers for Diverse Populations." In *Studying Teacher Education*, edited by M. Cochran-Smith and K. M. Zeichner, 477–548. Mahwah, NJ: Lawrence Erlbaum Associates.

hooks, b. 2014. *Feminism Is for Everybody: Passionate Politics*, second edition. New York: Routledge.

Hughes, C. 2002. *Key Concepts in Feminist Theory and Research.* Thousand Oaks, CA: Sage Publications.

Hutcheson, T. H. 2007. "The Truman Commission Vision of the Future." *NEA Thought and Action Higher Education Journal*, 107–115. Retrieved March 15, 2016 from http://www.nea.org/assets/img/PubThoughtAndAction/TAA_07_11.pdf.

Ignash, J. M. 1995. "Encouraging ESL Student Persistence: The Influence of Policy on Curricular Design." *Community College Review* 23 (3): 17–34. http://dx.doi.org/10.1177/009155219502300303.

Jalomo, R. E. Jr., and L. I. Rendón. 2004. "The Upside and Downside of the Transition to College." In *Transforming the First Year of College for Students of Color* (Monograph No. 38), edited by L. I. Rendón, M. García, and D. Person, 37–52. Columbia, SC: University of South Carolina, National Resource Center for the First-Year Experience and Students in Transition.

Johnston, T., and J. Old. 2011. *Navigating from Spanish to English.* Sandy, UT: Echo House Publishing.

———. 2015. *English Beyond the Basics: A Handbook for All Basic Writers with Assistance for Spanish Speakers*, fourth edition. Dubuque, IA: Kendall Hunt Publishing.

Jones, S. R. 2002. "(Re) Writing the Word: Methodological Strategies and Issues in Qualitative Research." *Journal of College Student Development* 43 (4): 461–73.

Kabat-Zinn, J. 2012. *Mindfulness for Beginners. Reclaiming the Present Moment—and Your Life.* Boulder, CO: Sounds True.

Kidd, S. M. 2003. *The Secret Life of Bees.* New York: Penguin Books.

Knight, M. G. 2004. "Sensing the Urgency: Envisioning a Black Humanist Vision of Care in Teacher Education." *Race, Ethnicity, and Education* 7 (3): 211–27. http://dx.doi.org/10.1080/1361332042000257047.

Krogstad, J. M. 2015. *5 Facts about Latinos and Education.* Washington, DC: Pew Hispanic Center. Retrieved January 10, 2016 from http://www.pewresearch.org/fact-tank/2015/05/26/5-facts-about-latinos-and-education/.

Krogstad, J. M., and R. Fry. 2015. *More Hispanics, Blacks, Enrolling in College, but Lag in Bachelor's Degree*. Washington, DC: Pew Hispanic Center. Retrieved February 23, 2016 from http://www.pewresearch.org/fact-tank/2014/04/24/more-hispanics-blacks-enrolling-in-college-but-lag-in-bachelors-degrees/.

Kumashiro, K. 2002. *Troubling Education: Queer Activism and Anti-Oppressive Pedagogy*. New York: Routledge Falmer Press.

Kurlaender, M. 2006. "Choosing Community College: Factors Affecting Latino College Choice." *New Directions for Community Colleges* 133: 7–16. http://dx.doi.org/10.1002/cc.223.

Laden, B. V. 1999. "Celebratory Socialization of Culturally Diverse Students through Academic Programs and Support Services." In *Community Colleges as Cultural Texts: Qualitative Explorations of Organizational and Student Culture*, edited by K. M. Shaw, J. R. Valadez, and R. A. Rhoads, 173–94. Albany, NY: SUNY Press.

Ladson-Billings, G. 1994. *The Dreamkeepers: Successful Teachers of African American Children*. San Francisco, CA: Jossey Bass.

———. 2001. *Crossing over to Canaan: The Journey of New Teachers in Diverse Classrooms*. San Francisco, CA: Jossey-Bass.

Lambie, R. A., S. D. Leone, and C. Martin. 2002. "Fostering Resilience in Children and Youth." In *Counseling the Adolescent: Individual, Family, and School Interventions*, fourth edition, edited by J. Carlson and J. Lewis, 87–119. Denver, CO: Love Publishing Company.

Levine, J. L., N. S. Shapiro, et al. 2004. *Sustaining and Improving Learning Communities*. San Francisco, CA: Jossey-Bass.

Lewis, M. G. 1998. "Foreword." In *Feminist Teaching in Theory and Practice: Situating Power and Knowledge in Poststructural Classrooms*, edited by B. Ropers-Huilman, xiii–xvi. New York: Teachers College Press.

Lipman, P. 1998. *Race, Class, and Power in School Restructuring*. Albany, NY: SUNY Press.

Lopez, M. H., and R. Fry. 2013. *Among Recent High School Grads, Hispanic College Enrollment Rate Surpasses That of Whites*. Washington, DC: Pew Hispanic Center. Retrieved March 23, 2016 from http://www.pewresearch.org/fact-tank/2013/09/04/hispanic-college-enrollment-rate-surpasses-whites-for-the-first-time/#comments.

Lorde, A. 1997. *The Collected Poems of Audre Lorde*. New York: W. W. Norton & Co. Inc.

Luskin, F. 2003. *Forgive for Good: A Proven Prescription for Health and Happiness*. New York: HarperOne Publishers.

Luthar, S. S., and L. B. Zelazo. 2003. "Research on Resilience: An Integrative Review." In *Resilience and Vulnerability: Adaptation in the Context of Childhood Adversities*, edited by S. S. Luthar, 510–49. Cambridge, UK: Cambridge University Press.

Lyubomirsky, S. 2007. *The How of Happiness: A New Approach to Getting the Life You Want*. New York: Penguin Press.

Maher, F. A., and M. K. T. Tetrault. 2001. *The Feminist Classroom: Dynamics of Gender, Race, and Privilege*. Lanham, MD: Rowman & Littlefield.

Martin, A. 2002. "Motivation and Academic Resilience: Developing a Model for Student Enhancement." *Australian Journal of Education* 46 (1): 34–49. http://dx.doi.org/10.1177/000494410204600104.

Martinez, M., and E. Fernández. 2004. "Latinos at Community Colleges." *New Directions for Student Services* 105: 51–62. http://dx.doi.org/10.1002/ss.116.

Masten, A., and D. Coatsworth. 1998. "The Development of Competence in Favorable and Unfavorable Environments: Lessons from Research on Successful Children." *American Psychologist* 53 (2): 205–20. http://dx.doi.org/10.1037/003-066X.53.2.205.

Mattoon, M. A. 2005. *Jung and the Human Psyche: An Understandable Introduction*: New York: Routledge.

Melguizo, T. 2009. "Are Community Colleges an Alternative Path for Mexican American Students to Attain a Bachelor's Degree?" *Teacher's College Record* 111 (1): 90–123. http://www.tcrecord.org/search.asp?kw=Melguizo&x=30&y=12.

Merriam, S. B. 1998. *Qualitative Research and Case Study Applications in Education*. San Francisco, CA: Jossey-Bass Inc.

————. 2009. *Qualitative Research: A Guide to Design and Implementation.* San Francisco, CA: Jossey-Bass Inc.

Minkler, J. E. 2002. "ERIC Review: Learning Communities at the Community College." *Community College Review* 30 (3): 46–63. http://dx.doi.org/10.1177/009155210203000304.

Moll, L., C. Amanti, D. Neff, and N. González. 2005. "Funds of Knowledge for Teaching: Using a Qualitative Approach to Connect Homes and Classrooms." In *Funds of Knowledge: Theorizing Practices in Households, Communities, and Classrooms,* edited by N. González, L. C. Moll, and C. Amanti, 71–87. Mahwah, NJ: Lawrence Erlbaum Associates.

Morales, E. E. 2000. "A Contextual Understanding of the Process of Educational Resilience: High Achieving Dominican American Students and the 'Resilience Cycle.'" *Innovative Higher Education* 23 (1): 7–22. http://dx.doi.org/10.1023/A:1007580217973.

————. 2013. *How to Be a Rubber Band: A Formula for Living Resilience Every Day.* Upper Saddle River, NJ: In Touch Press.

Muhammad J. S. 1995. "Mexico and Central America." In *No Longer Visible: Afro Latin Americans Today,* edited by Minority Rights Group, 163–79. Minority Rights Group.

National Center for Education Statistics. N.d. *Fast Facts: Race/Ethnicity of College Faculty.* Retrieved March 15, 2016 from http://nces.ed.gov/fastfacts/display.asp?id=61.

Nieto, S. 2004. "Toward an Understanding of School Achievement." In *Affirming Diversity: The Sociopolitical Context of Multicultural Education,* fourth edition, 254–303. Boston: Pearson Education Inc.

O'Gara, L., M. M. Karp, and K. L. Hughes. 2008, May. *Student Success Courses in the Community College: An Exploratory Study of Student Perspectives* (CCRC Working Paper No. 11). New York: Columbia University, Teachers College, Community College Research Center.

Palmer, P. J. 1998. *The Courage to Teach: Exploring the Inner Landscape of a Teacher's Life.* San Francisco, CA: Jossey-Bass.

Patton, M. Q. 2002. *Qualitative Research and Evaluation Methods,* third edition. Thousand Oaks, CA: Sage.

Post, S. G. 2011. *The Hidden Gifts of Helping: How the Power of Giving, Compassion, and Hope Can Get Us through Hard Times.* San Francisco, CA: Jossey-Bass.

Pratt-Johnson, Y. 2006. "Community College ESL Instructor: Jill of All Trades." In *Perspectives on Community College ESL: Vol. 2. Students, Mission, and Advocacy,* edited by C. Machado and A. Blumenthal, 87–100. Alexandria, VA: Teachers of English to Speakers of Other Languages, Inc.

Ramos, J. 2003. *The Other Face of America: Chronicles of the Immigrants Shaping Our Future.* New York: Harper Perennial.

Reinharz, S. 1992. "Conclusions." In *Feminist Methods in Social Research,* 240–69. New York: Oxford University Press.

Reis, S. M., R. D. Colbert, and T. P. Hébert. 2005. "Understanding Resilience in Diverse, Talented Students in an Urban High School." *Roeper Review* 27 (2): 110–20.

Rendón, L. I. 1994. "Validating Culturally Diverse Students: Toward a New Model of Learning and Student Development." *Innovative Higher Education* 19 (1): 33–50. http://dx.doi.org/10.1007/BF01191156.

————. 1999. *Fulfilling the Promise of Access and Opportunity: Toward a Vision of Collaborative Community Colleges for the 21st Century.* A Project of the W. K. Kellogg Foundation, American Association of Community Colleges, and Association of Community College Trustees. Retrieved May 16, 2007 from http://www.aacc.nche.edu/Resources/aaccprograms/pastprojects/Pages/fulfillingthepromise.aspx.

————. 2000. "Academics of the Heart." *About Campus* 5 (3): 3–5. http://dx.doi.org/10.1353/rhe.2000.0024.

————. 2002. "Community College Puente: A Validating Model of Education." *Educational Policy* 16 (4): 642–67. http://dx.doi.org/10.1177/0895904802016004010.

Rendón, L. I., M. García, and D. Person. 2004. "A Call for Transformation." In *Transforming the First Year of College for Students of Color* (Monograph No. 38), edited by L. I. Rendón, M. García, and D. Person, 3–22, 37, 42. Columbia, SC: University of South Carolina, National Resource Center for the First-Year Experience and Students in Transition.

Reyes, J. A., and M. J. Elias. 2011. "Fostering Social-Emotional Resilience among Latino Youth." *Psychology in the Schools* 48 (7): 723–27. http://dx.doi.org/10.1002/pits.20580.

Robinson, K. 2013. *Finding Your Element. How to Discover Your Talents and Passions and Transform Your Life*. New York: Viking.

Ropers-Huilman, B. 1998. *Feminist Teaching in Theory and Practice: Situating Power and Knowledge in Poststructural Classrooms*. New York: Teachers College Press.

Rolón, C. A. 2003. "Educating Latino Students." *Educational Leadership* 60 (4): 40–43.

Rutter, M. 1987. "Psychosocial Resilience and Protective Mechanisms." *American Journal of Orthopsychiatry* 57: 316–31.

Saleebey, D. 2006. "The Strengths Perspective: Possibilities and Problems." In *The Strengths Perspective in Social Work Practice*, fourth edition, edited by D. Saleebey, 279–303. New York: Pearson Allyn and Bacon.

Sandberg, S. 2013. *Lean In: Women, Work, and the Will to Lead*. New York: Knopf.

Sanders, W. L., and J. C. Rivers. 1996. *Cumulative and Residual Effects of Teachers on Future Student Academic Achievement*. Knoxville: University of Tennessee Value Added Research and Assessment Center.

Schuetz, P. 2002. *Challenges for Community Colleges*. Los Angeles, CA: ERIC Clearinghouse for Community Colleges. (ERIC Document Reproduction Service No. ED477829)

Seligman, M. E. P. 1998. "Building Human Strengths: Psychology's Forgotten Misión." *APA Monitor* 29 (1).

Shapiro, J. P. 1992. "What Is Feminist Assessment?" In *Students at the Center: Feminist Assessment*, edited by C. M. Musil, 29–38. San Francisco, CA: Association of American Colleges.

Shapiro, N. S., and J. H. Levine. 1999. *Creating Learning Communities: A Practical Guide to Winning Support, Organizing for Change, and Implementing Programs*. San Francisco, CA: Jossey-Bass.

Sherfield, R. M., R. J. Montgomery, and P. G. Moody. 2004. *Cornerstone: Building on Your Best*, fourth edition. Upper Saddle River, NJ: Prentice Hall.

Simonton, D. K. 2000. "Cognitive, Personal, Development, and Social Aspects." *American Psychologist* 55 (1): 151–58.

Smith, R. A. 2010. "Feeling Supported: Curricular Learning Communities for Basic Skills Courses and Students Who Speak English as a Second Language." *Community College Review* 37 (3): 261–84. http://dx.doi.org/10.1177/0091552109356592.

Snyder, C., and S. Lopez, eds. 2007. *Handbook of Positive Psychology*. New York: Oxford University Press.

Somers, P., K. Haines, and B. Keene. 2006. "Towards a Theory of Choice for Community College Students." *Community College Journal of Research and Practice* 30: 53–67.

Sroufe, A. L., B. Egeland, E. A. Carlson, and W. A. Collins. 2005. *The Development of the Person: The Minnesota Study of Risk and Adaptation from Birth to Adulthood*. New York: Guilford Press.

Stanton-Salazar, R. D. 2001. *Manufacturing Hope and Despair*. New York: Oxford University Press.

———. 2004. "Social Capital among Working-Class Minority Students." In *School Connections: U.S. Mexican Youth and School Achievement*, edited by M. A. Gibson, P. Gándara, and J. Peterson Koyama, 18–38. New York: Teachers College Press.

Stepanek, J. 2009. *Messenger: The Legacy of Mattie J. T. Stepanek and Heartsongs*. New York: New American Library.

Stepanek, M. J. T. 2003. *Loving through Heartsongs*. New York: Hyperion.

Stovall, M. 2000. "Using Success Courses for Promoting Persistence and Completion." *New Directions for Community Colleges* 112: 45–54. http://dx.doi.org/10.1002/cc.11204.

Strauss, R. P., and E. A. Sawyer. 1986. "Some New Evidence on Teacher and Student Competencies." *Economics of Education Review* 5 (4): 41–48.

Swing, R. L. 2002. *Benchmarking First-Year Seminars: A National Study of Learning Outcomes*. Retrieved September 26, 2011 from www.fyfoundations.org/PC/Randy/FYI2002.pdf.

Thompson, L. Y., C. R. Snyder, L. Hoffman, S. T. Michael, H. N. Rasmussen, L. S. Billings et al. 2005. "Dispositional Forgiveness of Self, Others, and Situations: The Heartland Forgiveness Scale." *Journal of Personality* 73: 313–59.

Tolle, E. 2005. *A New Earth: Awakening to Your Life's Purpose.* New York: Penguin Group.

Valdés, G. 1996. *Con Respeto: Building the Distances between Culturally Diverse Families and Schools.* New York: Teachers College Press.

Valenzuela, A. 1999. *Subtractive Schooling: U.S.-Mexican Youth and the Politics of Caring.* Albany, NY: SUNY Press.

Vaughn, G. B. 2005. "(Over)Selling the Community College: What Price Access?" *The Chronicle of Higher Education*, B12.

Villenas, S. A., and D. E. Foley. 2002. "Chicano/Latino Critical Ethnography of Education: Cultural Productions from *La Frontera.*" In *Chicano School Failure and Success: Past Present and Future*, second edition, edited by R. R. Valencia, 195–226. New York: Routledge Falmer.

Villenas, S. A., F. E. Godinez, D. Delgado Bernal, and C. A. Elenes. 2006. "Chicana/Latinas Building Bridges: An Introduction." In *Chicana/Latina Education in Everyday Life: Feminista Perspectives on Pedagogy and Epistemology*, edited by D. Delgado Bernal, C. A. Elenes, F. E. Godinez, and S. Villenas, 1–9. Albany, NY: SUNY Press.

Villenas, S. A., and M. Moreno. 2001. "To *Valerse por Si Misma* between Race, Capitalism, and Patriarchy: Latina Mother-Daughter Pedagogies in North Carolina." *International Journal of Qualitative Studies in Education* 14 (5): 671–87.

Wang, M. C., G. D. Haertel, and H. J. Walberg. 1994. "Educational Resilience in Inner Cities." In *Educational Resilience in Inner-City America: Challenges and Prospects*, edited by M. C. Wang and E. W. Gordon, 45–72. Hillsdale, NJ: Lawrence Erlbaum Associates.

Wayman, J. C. 2002. "The Utility of Educational Resilience for Studying Degree Attainment in School Dropouts." *Journal of Educational Research* 95 (3): 167–78.

Wiesel, E. 2006. *Night.* New York: Hill and Wang.

Werner, E., and R. Smith. 1992. *Overcoming the Odds: High Risk Children from Birth to Adulthood.* New York: Cornell University Press.

———. 2001. *Journeys from Childhood to the Midlife: Risk, Resilience, and Recovery.* New York: Cornell University Press.

Wolin, S. J., and S. Wolin. 1993. *The Resilient Self: How Survivors of Troubled Families Rise Above Adversity.* New York: Villard Books.

———. 2007. "Shifting the 'At Risk' Paradigm." In *Resiliency in Action*, edited by N. Henderson, B. Benard, and N. Sharp-Light, 123–26. Ojai, CA: Resiliency in Action.

Yañez, R. 2003. *El Paso del Norte: Stories on the Border.* Reno: University of Nevada Press.

———. 2011. *Cross over Water.* Reno: University of Nevada Press.

Zavella, P. 1997. "Feminist Insider Dilemmas: Constructing Ethnic Identity with Chicana Informants." In *Situated Lives: Gender and Culture in Everyday Life*, edited by L. Lamphere, H. Ragoné, and P. Zavella, 42–61. New York: Routledge.

About the Author

Dr. Blanca Campa is Professor of Educational Psychology at El Paso Community College and works primarily with Mexican American students. She was born and raised in the modest *colonia* of Salvarcar, Chihuahua, in the hills overlooking Ciudad Juárez. When she was still a child, her family immigrated to El Paso, Texas, where she attended public schools, became fluent in English, and graduated from high school. Her studies at El Paso Community College prepared her for transfer to the University of Texas at El Paso, where she studied education. She has served as an elementary school teacher, high school counselor, college counselor, and professor.

While teaching in the public schools, Campa earned a Master's of Education in Guidance and Counseling. Following the completion of her degree, Campa passed the Texas certification for Licensed Professional Counselor. In 2001 she was hired by El Paso Community College as an academic counselor and in 2004 she received an appointment as associate professor of Educational Psychology. In 2008 Campa earned a doctorate in Curriculum and Instruction with a minor in Educational Psychology from New Mexico State University. Campa currently teaches first-year experience classes for incoming students and various psychology courses.

Campa exemplifies the resilience of Latino community college students in the United States. Her research and writing is directly connected to her teaching, counseling, and mentoring. Her dissertation, a qualitative study of Mexican American community college students, was a unique blend of counseling and critical feminist theory focusing on *critical resilience*. Driving her work is the hope that her findings will assist her and other community college faculty to interact more effectively with students and help more Mexican Americans succeed in their academic studies. Campa has published works in the *Hispanic Journal of Behavioral Sciences*, the *Community College Jour-*

nal of Research and Practice, and the *Journal of Educational and Developmental Psychology*. Her work on resilience adds a unique perspective to this growing field.

CPSIA information can be obtained
at www.ICGtesting.com
Printed in the USA
BVOW03*2018230217
476926BV00002B/6/P